REBIRTH OF A NATION?

REBIRTH
OF A
NATION?

Garth Lean

BLANDFORD PRESS

POOLE DORSET

First published in 1976 by Blandford Press Ltd
Link House, West Street, Poole, Dorset BH15 1LL

ISBN   0 7137 0789 5   Hardback
ISBN   0 7137 0790 9   Paperback

Set in Times Roman on an AM Comp/Set 500
Printed in Great Britain by Biddles of Guildford

AUTHOR'S NOTE

This is one of a number of books, following the Call to the Nation, which are appearing at about the same time—notably the official book, *Dear Archbishop...*, edited by Mr John Poulton with an introduction by Dr Coggan, and *Land of Hope and Glory*, by the Archbishop of York, a brief guide based on the Lord's Prayer for those trying to pray for the country. I look forward to reading both of these.

It was suggested to me that this book might be postponed until after the publication of the official book, and I readily agreed. I am grateful to my publisher for being willing to alter my title, as previously announced, and to delay publication.

This book is the responsibility of no one except myself. I hope it may play a part, however small, in clarifying the issues involved and in forwarding the Archbishops' initiative towards a better Britain.

GDL

Contents

Be steady. The Christian faith will surely revive in this kingdom. You shall see it though I shall not.

Samuel Wesley to his sons, John and Charles

The uttermost purity is the first requisite of establishing social reform. No one who lacks moral purity is qualified to lead a crusade against evil social restrictions.

Mahatma Gandhi

1
Archbishops' move

Dr Coggan is a bold man. Together with his comrade of York he has called the British nation to face the moral problems underlying all our other troubles. And to remedy them.

This, you may say, is a natural thing for an Archbishop of Canterbury to do. Indeed, Mr Harold Macmillan, when asked as Prime Minister to give the nation a moral lead, declined to do so. He left all that to the Archbishop, he said. Instead he went on to win an election on the slogan, 'You never had it so good', while his Ministry waded through the Vassall and Profumo affairs.

The then Archbishop, Dr Geoffrey Fisher, did not take the hint, nor did his successor, Dr Ramsey, feel able to do so. They did many good things in the fields of ecumenism and world affairs, and Dr Ramsey, in particular, said repeatedly that economic problems were at base moral. They also took defensive steps against the theological wing of the New Morality when it reared its head, notably in the Southwark Diocese. But neither undertook any major attempt to reverse the tide of moral decline.

For moral decline there has been, however much the pundits may rage together. The new morality, which some of us thought very much like the old immorality excused, was at the outset a mainly sexual revolt. Its protagonists were apt to call it 'the sexual revolution' and to glory in the renaissance of the arts which they felt must

9

inevitably follow. Its clerical appeasers, too, seemed to concentrate largely on this sexual side of things—discussing when premarital intercourse was praiseworthy, when fornication 'proclaims the glory of God',[1] when adultery is portrayed as 'an act of holy communion'[2] and so on.

Alas, the renaissance of the arts has not followed, but only a great increase in the volume and savagery of pornography. And those who risked being called 'sex-obsessed' by saying that chastity was important, have seen what they feared come to pass.

Human life is all of a piece and when Christian standards are abandoned in one sphere, they are soon thought unnecessary in others. At about this time, I heard a discussion between two dons about whether it was permissible to seduce a girl in a tutorial. 'It is absurd to waste the opportunity,' said one. 'No,' said the other. 'Not in a tutorial. That would not be honest.' Now, alas, there are signs that honesty is suffering the same fate as chastity was suffering ten years ago. We are in the midst of a dishonesty revolution.

Nine tenths of London schoolchildren, we are told by Professor Belsen, have stolen more than trivially before they are sixteen, and the average boy will have stolen a hundred times before leaving school.[3] And in this they are imitating their elders. Some say that the nation of shopkeepers is becoming a nation of shoplifters and Dr James Ditton, a senior research fellow at Durham University, estimates that blue collar workers alone fiddle to the tune of £1,305 million a year,[4] a sum which takes no account of dishonesty by management, white collar workers, tax evasion or the public at large. Any of these estimates may be exaggerated, but the Poulson and T Dan Smith affairs show that large sums are involved and that it can be done by people so like the rest of us that men as supposedly shrewd as Edward Short and Reginald Maudling think them respectable colleagues.

We are also in the hate revolution. Seldom or never has the 'we-they' attitude been so widespread, nor its expression so violent. Ulster is a by-word, but *The Observer* suggests that in Britain as a whole 'sectional interests have reached the stage which diplomatic relations reached in 1914'. 'The great bitterness in public attitudes on industrial relations,' it adds, 'derives from a complete misunderstanding, a total failure of minds to meet.'[5] This understanding gap, which manifests itself in race relations and between the English, Irish, Welsh and Scots, is particularly alarming because it leads on so naturally to fantasies and violence.

On the title page of our book, *The New Morality*, published in January 1964, Arnold Lunn and I placed some words by Dr Mark Gibbon:

'The truth is that civilisation collapses when the essential reverence for absolute values which religion gives disappears. Rome had discovered that in the days of her decadence. Men live on the accumulated Faith of the past as well as on its accumulated self-discipline. Overthrow these and nothing seems missing at first, a few sexual taboos, a little of the prejudice of a Cato, a few rhapsodical impulses—comprehensible, we are told, only in the literature of folk lore—these have gone by the board. But something has gone as well, the mortar which held a society together, the integrity of the individual soul; then the rats come out of their holes and begin burrowing under the foundations and there is nothing to withstand them.'[6]

This process is now much further advanced and is becoming that 'surrender to materialism' which Alexander

Solzhenitsyn sees as bringing our country 'to the verge of a collapse by its own hands'.[7]

Whether Mr Macmillan, as a politician in office, was wise to forego any attempt to reverse this process, I do not know. Since his retirement he has attributed our troubles to the abandonment of 'the brotherhood of man under the fatherhood of God'. But as the Archbishop of York, Dr Stuart Blanch, has pointed out it may be 'asking a bit much of our political leaders to manage the sensitive and complicated machinery of government and at the same time to make their presence felt for good in every home, in every shop floor and in every office in the land'.[8]

Whether the previous Primates were right to hold their peace is also debatable. Perhaps they considered their years at Canterbury to be the wrong time to start a crusade—or a constructive debate.

Many, of course, and most of them churchmen, are even now saying that the Archbishops' timing is at fault. One has declared that since Bishop Gore thought a Call to be untimely sixty years ago, it is unnecessary today. But is there ever a convenient time for courage—for exposing oneself safely to the risk of failure? And the risk is there. For the gap between the Church, my church, and the people, has become almost as yawning wide today as it was in the early eighteenth century before Wesley.

The Archbishops' Call was, Dr Blanch tells us, made at the suggestion of politicians who are beginning to admit the nature and the urgency of the situation. Whether it was suggested by Mr Wilson himself, I cannot say, but it is known that he went to great lengths to obtain Dr Coggan's services at Canterbury. Dr Coggan, then 65, had been looking forward to retiring to a cottage in Yorkshire, and it took repeated and varied invitations, and much heart-searching on his own part, before he accepted. This self-sacrifice, together with his voluntary cut in salary, gave him a sound position from which to challenge the rest of us.

The appeal was prepared with the co-operation of the media and reached an unprecedented proportion of the nation. It became immediately apparent that it had not made the Archbishops popular in all quarters, and they will become much more unpopular yet, if they carry it through. For many who at first applauded will change their tune when the talking has to stop and the action begin. Change is seldom popular, when it is you who have to change—and no one is exempt if our country is to be reborn.

The importance of this attempt is more than national. All the democracies are in some kind of trouble. Many are facing economic problems not unlike our own. America has been shaken by a series of moral cataclysms which has left the Free World almost leaderless, and nearly every free country is a prey to violence stemming from sectional discord. If we can find the moral and spiritual rebirth which all, except ourselves, perceive that we need, others would be encouraged. If we fail, and our democratic institutions founder, the shock will be world-wide.

The Archbishops have asked for suggestions on how their call can be followed up by us all. I will try, in this book, to throw in my pennyworth. But first it is worth recalling what they have said—and how it has been received.

2

What they said

Dr Coggan launched his Call on 15 October 1975 with a press conference at Lambeth Palace. In the next few days he and Dr Blanch took part in thirteen national television and radio programmes, and on the following Sunday a pastoral letter from them both was read in all Anglican churches.

The Times headlined its account of Dr Coggan's activities: 'Archbishop urges nation to renew sense of moral purpose. "Materialism offers no solution." ' The fullest account was, perhaps, given by *The Daily Telegraph*[1] which reads:

The country is suffering from guzzling, grabbing and envy, and is without an anchor, drifting towards chaos, Dr Coggan said in a message to the nation from Lambeth Palace yesterday.

'I want to speak not only to members of the churches,' he said, 'but to all those who are concerned for the welfare of our nation at a time when many thoughtful people feel that we are drifting towards chaos.

'Many are realising that a materialistic answer is no real answer at all. There are moral and spiritual issues at stake.

'I believe the only creed that makes sense is: "God first—Others next—Self last".

'I see this worked out in the person and teaching of

Jesus Christ. He has shown us the way—He gives us the power to follow it.'

Addressing the enormous number of good people both inside and outside the churches, Dr Coggan stressed that he was not offering a blueprint for a way out of trouble.

But he wanted to see groups of men and women, of all denominations and of none, who would sit down and face the questions of what sort of society they wanted and what sort of people they needed to be in order to achieve it. Those interested in his approach to the nation's problems should write to him at Lambeth Palace, said Dr Coggan.

In all Anglican parish churches on Sunday, a pastoral letter was read from the Archbishop of Canterbury and the Archbishop of York. The letter calls on all Anglicans 'to pray steadily, persistently and intelligently for our nation and to live out the faith we profess that God reigns and God cares'.

In the press conference statement Dr Coggan said: 'Part of our trouble today is that we think the individual is powerless. This is a lie. He is not powerless.

'Each man and woman matters.

'Each man and woman counts. Your vote counts. Your voice counts. You count. Each man and woman is needed if the drift towards chaos is to stop. Your country needs you.

'The family matters.

'Give us strong, happy, disciplined families, and we shall be well on the way to a strong nation. The best way to cut at the roots of a healthy society is to undermine the family. So many young people who get into trouble with the law come from broken homes. The family matters, and it's worth working hard to build it, protect it and provide for it.

15

'Good work matters.

'A good day's work for a fair day's pay isn't a bad motto for worker and for management. But pay isn't everything. "Each for himself and the devil take the hindmost" makes for chaos. Guzzling doesn't satisfy. Grabbing and getting is a poor creed. Envy is a cancer. Sacrifice is an unpopular word; discipline even more so.

'But without sacrifice, without discipline, and without a sense of responsibility at the heart of our society, we're likely to perish. A bit of hardship hurts none of us. Can you deny it? We're growing soft.

'Attitudes matter.

'Of course we need money. We must think about money, but if we think about nothing else except money—and we are getting dangerously near to that sorry state today—the standards of our life will decline. Yes, even in the material sphere.

'Stark materialism does not work. It doesn't deliver the goods.

'We must adopt a different attitude to money, and to materials, and to machines. They are useful servants but they are degrading masters. It is the kind of people who handle them that matters and what their attitudes to life are. So stop making money the priority.'

Dr Coggan said that he had been in touch with the three main political party leaders in connection with his national Call, and had received letters from two of them. He refused to say which one had not yet replied.

He also had the wholehearted goodwill of the Roman Catholic and Free churches.

Dr Coggan said: 'Most serious-minded people realise that our economic problems are bound to deeper ones. I think we have failed in recent times to discover the problems behind our economic distress.

'It is very interesting to find how many people from all strata of society are very deeply concerned at the state of our society at the moment.

'It was an American politician who said that Britain has lost an empire and not found a role. Perhaps it would also be true to suggest that Britain has lost an empire and has not found her soul.'

Dr Coggan said there were constant news stories of declining church membership, and it was true that the church was facing economic difficulties like everybody else. But it was still able to give a fillip, encouragement and some leadership to people.

He hoped his appeal would not bring bitterness from any section of the community, particularly the one and a quarter million unemployed. 'The most degrading thing that can happen to a man is to feel he is unwanted. If there is bitterness from the unemployed I hope they know they have my deepest sympathy.'

Dr Stuart Blanch, the Archbishop of York, made the following statement, which he headed 'Aims for Britain':

'The Archbishops are not offering an easy solution to the nation's problems because there is no easy solution. Their aims are:

'1. To ask people to face up to the basic question—"What sort of society do we want?"—and to stimulate thought and discussion about it.

'2. To test public opinion to see whether any moral or social consensus exists and, if so, to help people to express it at the national and local level.

'3. To mobilise our spiritual resources within and outside the Christian churches in pursuit of a less divided and more satisfying corporate life—not only for our own nation but for mankind as a whole.'[2]

Later Dr Coggan suggested five areas which might be considered by people and groups discussing the Archbishops' two main questions:

Employment and the right attitude to work
Reconciling law and order with freedom
Power and powerlessness and God's power
How enterprise can exist without selfishness
Integrity at all levels—personal, social and political.[3]

3
The great debate

The Archbishops' Call aroused an immediate response. Thousands of letters—at first four to five thousand a day—poured into Lambeth, almost all favourable. When Dr Coggan appeared at a city church a few days later, it was crammed and five hundred people applauded him as he left. 'Instead of dispersing,' reported *The Daily Telegraph*, 'the crowd moved, increasing in size as it did so, into Cheapside to wait the Archbishop's departure. It was noticeable that many young people were there, apparently eager to express their support.'[1]

Some of Dr Coggan's television encounters went less smoothly. When he met the President of the Municipal and General Workers' Union, David Basnett, and Sir Frederick Catherwood, it became apparent that neither thought much alteration necessary in their own people. Basnett did not think union leaders could ask further sacrifices from their members and Sir Frederick, having said that managers, being responsible people, naturally welcomed but hardly needed the call, went on to lecture the Primate on the insufficiently Christian content of his message.

When Colin Morris conducted Dr Coggan to a factory, the workers were friendly but each and every one said that the call would make no difference to the way he or she lived. A group of parents, to whom Morris then conducted him, were more lively. Some were vehemently hostile to any suggestion that family life or parental behaviour could be improved, while others no less strongly supported Dr Coggan. Here was a real debate, though again no-one suggested that his own behaviour would be different.

Meanwhile, controversy raged in the Press. The *Methodist Recorder* gave generous support, while hoping, as did leaders of the Jewish and Buddhist communities, that they would not be left out. A canon, noting that the Archbishop appealed to the whole nation, considered his formulation 'God first, others next, self last' a failure to take serious unbelief seriously. *The Church Times* objected to the Archbishop's emphasis on getting 'people asking questions rather than giving them answers' and quoted back at him his earlier statement that 'many have lost their faith in any positive proclamation of the Gospel' and 'can do little more than ask questions'. It wondered whether 'this is the kind of pastoral letter, muted and inoffensive, which St Paul would have issued in the circumstances'.[2]

Not everyone, however, seemed to find the letter inoffensive. *The Daily Telegraph* wrote it off as 'over-simplification' and said that Dr Coggan 'should leave to Caesar the things that are his'. 'The fact of a moral and spiritual malaise is one thing: on this the Church ought to speak vigorously. It is wrong all the same to imply that there is any direct and necessary connection between these matters and the economic position of Britain.'[3]

More deeply offended were the Jubilee Group of Anglo-Catholic clergy who said the Call showed 'a most appalling failure to understand the position of families under economic stress at a time of high unemployment' and was 'characterised by its attempt to preserve peace and a stable society in the face of chaos'.[4] Some of these clergy privately spoke of it as 'moral guff', and attacked Dr Coggan in a series of sermons and newspaper articles.

'Both the letter and the statement are an attempt to moralise within the accepted framework of capitalism,' wrote one of the Group's founders, the Rev Kenneth Leech. 'What is now abundantly clear is that the fundamental cleavage within the Christian world is between those who see the Christian social witness in terms of defence of an established social order from the past and those who see the Spirit of God working through the political upheavals of the present, working judgment in the midst of the earth.'[4]

The Daily Telegraph and the Jubilee Group each make a point, but is either *the* point?

The Daily Telegraph rightly says that there are technical economic decisions to be made—the level of taxation, for example, and whether to nationalise the aircraft industry—on which the Church cannot speak with any special authority. But does that prove that our 'moral and spiritual malaise' has 'no direct and necessary connection' with Britain's economic position?

The Labour MP for Warley East, Mr Andrew Faulds, points out that 'thought for others before self' is 'of crucial importance in terms of social relationships, the bloodstream of the body politic'. 'We politicians,' he adds, 'play on self-interest to boost our electoral chances. Both great parties have become even more promoters and prisoners of sectional interests. We have helped create a climate where there is a ready claim to rights and less readiness to serve, whether we are doctors or dockers. So much of our present plight flows from the fact that we are me-firsters.'[5] Is not this equally true of the rest of us?

Surely *The Times* was right, as long ago as 1963, to write that 'unless the issue is regarded by both

21

Government and Opposition and eventually by the greater part of the nation, as a moral one, the battle is unlikely to be won.' More recently it added, 'We need nothing less than a revolution in the spirit of the nation.'[6] Sir John Lawrence put it well in *Take Hold of Change*: 'From one aspect,' he writes, 'our problems are economic and social, but they are also moral and spiritual. We make them insoluble if we try to separate these two aspects.'[7]

Equally one respects the passion for justice displayed by Father Kenneth Leech and his friends, especially as some of them, like Bishop Winter, have suffered for their beliefs. But is it not a trifle arrogant to write off everyone who does not agree with one's own particular nostrums as a capitalist lackey?

Dr Coggan, for one, has as good a record as most in caring for the less fortunate, at home and abroad, and has been much attacked for it. When, two weeks after moving to Canterbury, he told the Synod that 'patriotism was a travesty if it put country before the needs of others, including the Third World' and challenged Britain to meet the UN Aid target of 0.7% of our GNP, Mr Enoch Powell attacked him for talking 'dangerous nonsense' and advocating 'tyranny with a halo of Christianity'.[8]

Father Leech, alas, does tend to divide his fellow Christians into 'goodies' and 'badies', and the 'goodies' are apt to be few and far between. For example, he maintains that 'Anglo-Catholicism is the only form in which Christianity can and ought to survive in the modern world,' which must be one of the most sweeping excommunications in history. And not even most Anglo-Catholics get through his sieve. In the same article, he complains that much of the Anglo-Catholic movement, especially in London, has become little more than 'lace, gin and backbiting' and is 'enough to turn people off

Christianity for good'.[9] Everyone out of step except our Kenneth?

There can be no doubt, however, that Dr Coggan had struck a note which echoed in thousands of hearts. *The Guardian* quoted a survey confirming his diagnosis:

'The claim of Dr Coggan that many people feel they are drifting, lost in insecurity and uncertainty, is supported. ... Insecurity and anxiety are verging on disillusionment and fear. Those have led in turn to bewilderment and a great sense of powerlessness.

'Disillusionment, at least among the older people, seemed frequently to be a deep disappointment at the apparent failure of their earlier idealism and hopes for social reform. They mentioned the ills of affluence or its fragility, the elusiveness of social justice, or the threats to social order. "For both young and old, it was expressed in a retreat from politics."'[10]

The survey was conducted personally by members of the governing assembly of the British Council of Churches, but when the Council met for its autumn meeting their debate was widely reported as confused and disappointing. In the end the Council agreed that groups, including experts, should study 'some of the issues which cause problems' and report in about two years.

Meanwhile, by the year's end, 27,000 letters had reached Lambeth and 300 more were arriving each week. 70,000 prayer cards had been sent out, enough donations had been received to pay for postage and stationery and fifty volunteers had given their time for three months. Church attendance appeared to be up in many places and local groups were meeting to discuss the Archbishop's two main questions—'What kind of a society do we want?' and 'What kind of people do we need to be in order to achieve it?'

By late February, the Archbishop of York was able to claim that if the usual BBC formula were adopted and the number of letters actually written was multiplied by a hundred to give the number of those interested, you would have a figure of three million. 'I suppose,' he commented, 'it amounts to a conviction much more widely held than we may sometimes assume, that the Christian way remains the ideal, though quite impracticable, way of managing our personal and our public affairs.... But perhaps it is not so impracticable after all.'

4

Southwark's red herrings

The most sensational, and in some ways helpful, intervention in early stages of the debate was the article by the Bishop of Southwark, Dr Mervyn Stockwood in the Communist *Morning Star* on 1 October. It was sensational coming from a senior diocesan bishop and helpful in that it revived a dying publicity and provoked a controversy which defined issues more clearly.

The Bishop's thesis, pressed home with his usual flair, was that Dr Coggan overlooked that a man's character is 'partly if not largely determined by his environment, by the social and economic circumstances in which he is placed'. British society, an economic system which is based on selfishness and greed and which leads to class divisions, injustice and unemployment, was bound to produce social chaos. 'It is this system more than any other single factor, that is producing the evils that Dr Coggan so greatly deplores. If he is right in thinking that our country is heading for disaster, let him draw the attention of the nation to the system that is largely responsible for it.'

'Meanwhile,' concluded the Bishop with a flourish, 'I have no intention of shoring up a society which, because of its basic injustice, is at last crumbling in ruins.'

The Bishop confused matters by choosing the Communist newspaper for his intervention and by stating, by way of example, that 'if a Communist government were to be established in Britain, the West End would be cleared up overnight and the ugly features of our permissive society would be changed in a matter of days'. 'And then,' he concluded, 'heaven help the porn merchants and all engaged in the making of fortunes through the commercial exploitation of sex.'

The choice of paper, Dr Stockwood later explained, was due to his desire to defend the Archbishop from the *Morning Star*'s accusation of 'union-bashing', though it must be admitted that the article did not read like a defence. Why, when any paper of Fleet Street would have been open to him, did he choose to preach to the converted, to denounce British society, the Archbishop and capitalism to Communists rather than to readers of, say, the *Daily Express*, who, one would suppose, stood in greater need of his message?

But the message is more important than the medium, and it is astonishing that so old a controversialist as Dr Stockwood should have committed himself to that extraordinary commendation of Communist methods of repression. Every Christian should, indeed, be ashamed of the flaunting of sex for profit in our Western society, something which is not allowed in Russia. One recalls the embarrassment of Mr Antony Chenevix-Trench, then Headmaster of Eton, when an official of the Soviet Ministry of Education showed him 'a great English classic of absolutely impeccable morality', bound in a salacious cover[1] and asked him, 'Do you have to disguise your classics as pornography in order to sell them?'

One is glad to see that Dr Stockwood recognises that a film like *The Exorcist* 'may be a money-spinning film for the promoters, but has done immeasurable harm'. But, if censorship is the answer, as the Bishop seems to think, are the whip and the jack boot, leave alone the labour camp

26

and the mental hospital, what we need in Britain?

Much was written in the Press about whether Bishop Stockwood had just made a careless slip or whether he was really as favourable to Communist ideas as he made out to the readers of the *Morning Star*—and the intervention of *Izvestia* in his support further confused matters.[2] The clash sometimes became sharp. Pastor Richard Wurmbrand remarked that, when the Communists took over in Roumania an 'ugly feature' did indeed disappear overnight—'the existence of faithful bishops'. 'Absolutely all Catholic bishops were put in prison and tortured; and all but two died there,' he wrote.[3] Kenneth Leech, combining an undoubted truth with a gratuitous jibe, retorted that while 'dear Mervyn Stockwood' would be imprisoned in the Soviet Union, Dr Coggan 'would not because he is discreet and tactful and would no doubt fit into that system as into this'—and the jibe was repeated widely by Father Leech's friends.[4]

As far as the real national debate was concerned, all this was a red herring. The fundamental difference between the Archbishop and the Bishop was succinctly stated in a *Sunday Telegraph* leader:

'Dr Coggan holds that you have to change the individual before you can change and reform the injustices of society. Dr Stockwood contends that "a man's character, be it good or bad, is partly if not largely determined by his environment, by the social and economic circumstances in which he is placed". This comes very near to denying the individual the power to choose between right and wrong. There is no doubt which is the Christian view. It is one to which the communion of saints bears witness over the centuries.'[5]

It may be argued that this contrast is an over-simplification; Dr Coggan has often said that 'environment is a formative factor'. But he adds, 'Improvements in the environment do not necessarily make for better people. After all we have made enormous progress in our comforts these last two or three decades. But is ours a happier or more secure society?'[6]

Dr Stockwood, being a Christian, also does, I am sure, have faith that the grace of God can change individual character, whatever the circumstances. Yet research reveals that he and some of those closely associated with him have from time to time tended towards what might be called the New Predestination, the theory that men are powerless against their environment.

As long ago as July 1964 Dr Stockwood told the House of Lords that 'most of those in prison were there because society or their families had failed them'[7] and his then close associate, Dr John Robinson, described suicide as 'a sin of society against the individual rather than a sin of the individual against society'.[8] Other instances of this theory are given in *The Cult of Softness*, the second book in which Sir Arnold Lunn and I collaborated, and our research revealed too few cases in which the clerical new moralists, then centred in Southwark, stressed the power of God to change people. They seemed to be more anxious to change the Christian code to fit the conditions now prevailing, an exercise which they conducted in the name of compassion.

But is it compassionate for a clergyman to suggest that Jesus Christ cannot answer any and every problem? John Wesley rejected the Calvinist doctrine of Predestination because it represented God as 'more false, more cruel and more unjust than the devil, for it said that God had condemned millions of people to everlasting fire for continuing in sin, which for want of grace which He gives them not, they are unable to avoid'.[9] The New Predestination whereby neither human effort nor grace from God can enable us to improve seems scarcely less cruel or false. It is an even more blatant contradiction of the New Testament.

It is, also, a profoundly pessimistic attitude which undermines morality. For if we are led to think that our natures or our actions are 'determined' by social conditions or psychological drives, why should we resist temptation? We can excuse anything and everything we want to do by saying, 'society made me like that' or 'it's all because of my wretched childhood'—excuses by no means confined to the under privileged. 'A churchman,' commented *The Guardian* pithily, 'ought to know better than to suggest that society dictates personal morality.'[10]

Yet the New Predestination has to be taken seriously, for according to Clifford Longley, *The Times* Religious Correspondent, 'at least half of the church's forty-three diocesan bishops'—and they the younger half—agree with Dr Stockwood's general theme. 'Although it is unlikely that Dr Stockwood was acting as their spokesman in this attack, broadly speaking his criticisms would be theirs,' Mr Longley wrote. 'They consider the main thrust of Dr Coggan's remarks, against materialism and private greed, was misplaced. Many of them are known to believe that the fault lies with society rather than with individuals, and that the present economic system fosters and encourages ambition and material acquisitiveness.'[11]

The Bishop of Leicester somewhat undermined Mr Longley's claim in his letter to the paper. But if even a few bishops have lost their nerve to the extent that they think individuals powerless and society the cause of most sin, it is a matter for grave concern.

NOTE

A curious feature of Father Kenneth Leech's political philosophy is his attitude to films like *The Exorcist* or *Clockwork Orange*. Even while applauding Bishop Stockwood's *Morning Star* article, he paused to call the Bishop 'a kind of Stalinist version of Mrs Whitehouse' for saying *The Exorcist* had done 'immeasurable harm'. Of those who criticise *Clockwork Orange* —a film which has inspired many muggings and rapes, as well as at least one major United States assassination attempt—he writes, 'They (the critics) have played straight into the hands of those who wish to keep Christianity from being offensive in our grotesquely unjust society.'[12]

Bishop Trevor Huddleston, a man whom no one can accuse of complacent conservatism, specifically rejects this view and notes how strange it is that those who recognise most swiftly the offence against the dignity of man in racial and economic actions, fail altogether to recognise it at other levels. 'Pornography,' he says, 'is an abuse of that which is made in the likeness and image of God. Chastity is the condition for and the way to the Vision of God.'

'An inescapable element in the Christian calling,' Bishop Huddleston continues, 'is what we call Chastity: what Christ calls "purity of heart". This, so far from being a negative, pallid, kill-joy kind of calling, is the most positive of all responses to the "many-splendoured thing" which is life.'[13]

Mahatma Gandhi once remarked: 'The uttermost purity is the first requisite of establishing social reform. No one who lacks in moral purity is qualified to lead a crusade against evil social restrictions.'

5

The two atheisms

If, then, we reject the New Predestination, can we just ignore the social evils mentioned by Dr Stockwood in his *Morning Star* article? Certainly not, for, in spite of the welfare state, they exist, and are a scandal for which we are all responsible.

Dr Stockwood outlined them with obvious sincerity in *The Times* of 20 February 1974. Here are some extracts from that article:

'Few (in Britain) are starving but there are millions of people eking out desperately meagre and underprivileged lives. At one end of the scale there are extravagant riches and comfort; at the other end, poverty, hardship and squalor.

'If we were a homeless miner or a homeless anybody, what then would be our attitude to Centre Point which has allowed a speculator, under Labour and Conservative governments, to increase his capital from £5 million to £55 million in 10 years?

'What about the thousands and thousands of semi-literate, often violent, children who may become the most vicious and disruptive factor in our society, destroying so much of what we believe to be worthwhile and sacred?

'The housing situation is *worse* than when I became Bishop of Southwark fifteen years ago. Each year, no matter whether Conservative or Labour has been in control, the situation has deteriorated. Do you know, for instance, as you and I go to our comfortable beds, eight thousand Londoners are sleeping in the open and rough, each night? ...The question is directed not only to those who make vast profits through speculation but to those who ruthlessly demand an increase in wages, often by restrictive practices, which inevitably lead to such a wide-scale inflation that wrecks our economy.'

But who denies these facts? Certainly not Dr Coggan. He has worked on these social problems for years, and there is no reason to think that he is any less concerned about them than is Dr Stockwood.

Why then all the sound and fury? Why could not Dr Stockwood and his friends, Father Leech and the Rev Paul Oestreicher, have built on Dr Coggan's initiative instead of producing a newspaper confrontation?

The Observer put it down to Dr Stockwood being 'unable to resist showing off'. 'Southwark is a great opposer of the Establishment and is spurred on these days by his brand new honorary chaplain, the Rev Paul Oestreicher,'[1] it said.

A more powerful motive may have been that Dr Stockwood thought he should have been more fully consulted, and some other bishops are reported to have felt the same. This is understandable. But, if the Archbishop had consulted them all, the result, according to the Bishop of Wakefield, Dr Treacy, would have been chaos and stagnation. 'He would have been faced by forty-one differing opinions and doubtless a drafting committee would have been appointed.'[2]

Or perhaps Dr Stockwood just does not like calls. In his 20 February article, he wrote, 'As a Christian politician and a bishop, I have often been asked with others to call the country to a crusade, but I have always refused.' Fair enough. Why then, should he be consulted? And why muddy the stream when others are trying to fish?

The complaint that the Archbishops should have been more specific from the start and denounced the 'injustices of the system' is also an arguable point of view. But if they had done that, they would have been denouncing only a small part of the population rather than calling everyone to take part in the reformation of Britain. There is, of course, a duty to denounce injustice; but it can be an overpopular—even a self-indulgent—pastime. It excludes oneself from the need to change. Surely the Archbishops were right to begin by challenging every man, woman and child in Britain.

It is a sad fact that if one denounces 'the system', very few people feel concerned—although in a democracy, the system is all of us.

And even if the system was transformed, would that solve the problem? The Communists have always believed that human society would not be satisfactory until a new type of man has been created, and a leading Soviet ideologist described that new man as 'a person who has renewed himself with a new attitude towards work and social duties, with new moral standards, with a high measure of discipline and moral purity, with harmony between word and deed'[3]—not at all a bad answer to the Archbishops' second question.

This new man was to be created by changing the economic system. Shulubin, the old Communist in Solzhenitsyn's *Cancer Ward* says: 'We thought it was enough to change the mode of production and immediately people would change as well. But did they change? The hell they did. They did not change a bit.'[4]

A resolution of the 22nd Congress (1961) of the Soviet Communist Party seems to agree. 'The Party considers that the creation of the new man is the most difficult part of the Communist transformation of society,' it said. 'Unless we can root out bourgeois morality and educate people in Communist morality, renewing them morally and spiritually, it is not possible to build a Communist society.' And Krushchev later admitted, 'The contradictions in Communist society have their cause in the inability to make a selfless man.'

That is no reason for complacency about our own economic system. It certainly has not created the 'unselfish man', nor has it ever aimed to do so. If its whole history is considered, capitalism may have countenanced as much inhumanity as Communism, even if we face Solzhenitsyn's figure of 66 million killed in Russia alone. Though the 'ugly face of capitalism' has been considerably softened almost everywhere in recent decades, that system still plays its part in a world where 460 million people are 'actually starving' at this moment.

All the same, we in Britain would be mad to think that a change of system will automatically change everything. 'The difference between capitalism and Communism,' runs the grim joke current in Eastern Europe, 'is that under capitalism man exploits man, while under Communism it's the other way round.' Should we risk losing our liberties for that? 'Democracy,' someone said, 'is a bad form of government, but everything else so far invented is worse.' As *The Times* remarked in its editorial upon Dr Stockwood's *Morning Star* article: 'A free society will inevitably contain many evils, against which good and sincere men will struggle, but totalitarian rule does not only contain evils, it is evil.'[5]

Our British need is for reform by democratic means—and the creation of new men to initiate those reforms and carry them through. As a wise old Marxist, Hans Böckler, the first President of the German Trade Union Federation after the war, said: 'If men are to be free from the old and outmoded it can only happen as they set themselves a new goal, and place humanity and moral values first. When men change, the structure of society changes; and when the structure of society changes, men change. Both go together and both are necessary.'[6]

This is near to Dr Coggan's point. 'The truth is that we have to work at our problem from both ends, that is both trying to make better people and trying to make better structures of society,' he wrote, on 4 December. 'Because we have been paying too little attention to the first of these I started there, but not in order to finish there.'[7]

Malcolm Muggeridge has pointed out that Christianity involves a balanced obligation—towards God and our neighbour—and that few find that balance. St Simeon Stylites on his pillar 'loved God and would doubtless have claimed to love his neighbour, but perched up there he was too remote for this love to find any effective expression'. In our time, Muggeridge says, the balance has swung heavily the other way: 'St Simeon has come down from his pillar to become Comrade Simeon, the Rt Hon Simeon or Senator Simeon or just Sim, with God no more than a constitutionally elected President to perform ceremonial duties and deliver an address from the Throne.'[8] That way lies sterility, for if we confine our Christianity to politics, politics soon takes over. 'They who love you for political service,' said John Wesley, 'love you less than their dinner; and they that hate you, hate you worse than the Devil.'[9]

A Christian should, of course, be concerned with politics. But if he thinks politics by itself can create a new society, he is not only naive but getting perilously near to a practical atheism—the atheism which has lost the faith that God can intervene radically enough in the lives of individuals to alter their motives and public actions.

35

It is, however, equally atheistic, as Paul Oestreicher points out, to 'privatise religion',[10] to regard it as something designed solely to give an individual comfort or personal salvation. 'Next to losing a sense of a personal Christ,' wrote Professor Henry Drummond, the author of *Natural Law in the Spiritual World*, 'the worst evil which can befall a Christian is to have no sense of anything else. To grow up in a complacent belief that God has no business in this great groaning world of human beings except to attend to a few saved souls is the negation of all religion.'[11]

On the one hand, there is a social programme, with only remote Christian antecedents, which turns to that violence which Christ repudiated for His disciples. On the other is the ghetto philosophy which keeps personal faith intact, but does little or nothing to equip and re-motivate us to save the lives of millions of people faced with tyranny or starvation.

Both of these—and I have been subject to both—root in doubt of the power of God, and I have found that doubt and dirt often go together. I doubt the power of God when I am not allowing Him to work wonders in me—to clean up the dirt and make me new. Then, of course, there cease to be miracles of grace in me and around me.

The real Christian revolution is one that begins by transforming the self-centred motives of the individual and goes on to change his relationships with everyone. It is the overflowing of God's love into every corner and structure of society. It is, in fact, the operation of the power which raised Jesus from the dead, bringing the full dimension of change—social, national and international change, all based on personal change.

6
Men have changed conditions

But can a spiritual change in men really lead to a change in conditions? There are numerous examples in the history of most nations of how this has happened. An example from our own is the story of William Wilberforce and the abolition of the slave trade.[1]

In 1783 Wilberforce was poised at a point of rare opportunity. Although not a Minister he sat on the Government Front Bench and was perhaps the only attractive debater on whom the young Prime Minister, William Pitt, could rely in the unequal battle with North, Fox, Burke and their massive array of talent and numbers. He was Pitt's most intimate friend and had just won the County of Yorkshire seat for him in the teeth of the great families. He had become so considerable a figure that Pitt once offered to postpone the meeting of Parliament for ten days rather than face the session without him.

Pitt, son of the great Chatham and himself an orator in an age of orators, said Wilberforce had 'the greatest natural eloquence of all the men I ever knew'. He was called 'the nightingale of the House of Commons'. After he sang at the Duchess of Devonshire's ball of 1782, the Prince of Wales said he would go anywhere to hear him.

His voice was matched by his charm, and his charm by his wealth. His merchant uncle had left him a nine-bedroomed villa in Wimbledon, where Pitt lived with him for much of five years and where the 'grave young

Minister' was once found to have been up early sowing the flowerbeds with bits of a friend's opera hat. 'Hundreds of times I have roused Pitt out of bed and conversed with him while he was dressing. I was the repository of his most confidential thoughts,' Wilberforce said years later. They were 'exactly like brothers'.

So the two, identical in age and matched in brilliance, set out for high adventure together. At this moment an unexpected event took place. Wilberforce, in a matter of months, underwent a change of character which shattered most of his conceptions, and left him a new man, uncertain where his path would lead. This change was a result of the spiritual surge in Britain initiated by the Wesleys. Young Wilberforce, at the age of ten, had lived for some time with (in his mother's opinion) an over-zealous Methodist aunt in Wimbledon. His mother, fearful lest he be 'converted', removed him hastily to the gaieties of Hull, and ironically it was through this withdrawal that the delayed character change came to the rising young Member of Parliament. For, at Hull, he met a brilliant young schoolmaster, Isaac Milner, who was later to become Vice-Chancellor of Cambridge University and Dean of Carlisle. It was talks with Milner on a continental tour which led Wilberforce to a radical reappraisal of his life.

Back in London, his mind in a ferment, Wilberforce began his life-long habit of spending the first hours of the day with God. 'Began three or four days ago to get up very early,' he wrote on 25 October. 'In the solitude of the morning had some thoughts which I trust will come to something.' He began to keep a private journal, quite distinct from his diary. 'Began my journal with a view to make myself humble and watchful. Bacon says, "Great changes are easier than small ones",' was his first entry. In the next days, among many convictions of his own worthlessness and pleas for Christ's intervention, he set down the thoughts received. An early one was to 'go and converse with Mr Newton', the converted slave ship captain who was by then Rector of St Mary Woolnoth. After a week of struggle he obeyed, and that interview was a turning point. 'When I came away, I found my mind in a calm and tranquil state,' he wrote.

In his early morning hour, Wilberforce reviewed his public as well as his private life. 'The first years in Parliament I did nothing—nothing, I mean, to any purpose. My own distinction was my darling object.' And again, 'God Almighty has set before me two great objects, the suppression of the slave trade and the reformation of manners.'

England, at the time, was the world's leading slave-trading nation. Her ships sailed out of Liverpool, Bristol or London, for the West African coast and there, by direct seizure, purchase from Arab traders or barter with local chiefs, gathered their cargo. The men slaves were packed between decks, chained in pairs onto shelves with only two and a half feet headroom. Women and children, if not chained, were packed equally tight, with no room to lie down and exposed to the lusts of the crew. 300 to 600 would be the normal cargo for a ship of 100 to 150 tons. By the time they reached America or the West Indies, ten per cent would normally be dead, while another thirty or forty per cent would die soon after arrival under the process politely called 'seasoning'. An American authority estimates that Britain supplied three million slaves to the French, Spanish and British colonies before 1776.

'The Trade', as it was called, was not just another successful business, but national policy. Legalised by royal charters of 1631, 1633 and 1672, by an Act of Parliament in 1689 and by treaties in 1713, 1725 and 1748, 'no less a statesman than the Elder Pitt,' says Lecky, 'made its development a main object of his policy.' The most prized fruit of Marlborough's wars was the Asiento clause of the Treaty of Utrecht, by which Britain wrested from France and Spain the virtual monopoly of the slave trade with America. The Trade was not only the foundation of the British plantation industry in the West Indies (in which, according to the Duke of Clarence, a hundred million sterling was invested by 1799) but was considered essential as a training ground of sailors for the Navy.

A wide cross-section of the nation derived profit from it. Between 1783 and 1793 Liverpool slavers alone are said to have carried three hundred thousand slaves, selling them for over £15 million at a good profit. A number of seats in the House of Commons were controlled by men grown rich through slavery, but an even more powerful factor than the West Indian lobby was the feeling that change was dangerous to national interests, especially in time of war. Nelson's view was typical. He wrote from the *Victory*, 'I was bred in the good old school and taught to appreciate the value of our West Indian possessions, and neither in the field nor the Senate shall their just rights be infringed, while I have an arm to fight in their defence or a tongue to launch my voice against the damnable doctrine of Wilberforce and his hypocritical allies.'

The question of humanity did not arise in most people's minds, because slaves were regarded not as men, but as property. Thus, both sides in the *Zong* case of 1783 ignored the loss of 132 lives—thrown overboard by the owner to profit by his insurance. It was, said the Attorney General, 'a case of goods and chattels', 'a throwing of goods overboard to save the residue', and the law, said Chief Justice Mansfield, was 'exactly as if horses had been thrown overboard.' The Solicitor General deprecated the 'pretended appeals' to 'humanity' and agreed that the master had the unquestioned right to drown as many as he wished without 'any shew or suggestions of cruelty' or a 'surmise of impropriety'.

Lord St Vincent perhaps got nearest to expressing the secret feelings of the comfortable classes when he cautioned the House of Lords against setting up 'what was right' against 'what was established'. 'The whole fabric of society would go to pieces if the wedge of abstract right were once entered into any part of it,' he said.

It was this stubborn opposition which deterred the great men in the Commons from taking up the issue. Burke, the 'political moralist', had been convinced of the injustice of the Trade since 1772, but did not proceed for fear that 'the strength of the West Indian body would defeat the utmost efforts of his party and cover them with a ruinous unpopularity'. Pitt dared not take the lead, because the King and the Royal Family, as well as most of his cabinet, were against it. Any man who dared focus the issue in his person would say goodbye to high office.

Wilberforce put down his first motion against the Trade in 1787. It was to be a twenty-year battle. Every year except three—between 1800 and 1803—he brought the matter up in the House. Each year, while they lived, Pitt and Fox stood with him, though there were times when Pitt, faced with a critical war situation and a divided cabinet, seemed to his watchful friend a little weary in well-doing. Disappointment was frequent. When in 1797 the advances of the previous year were wiped out—he was voted down by 74 to 70 while twelve of his pledged supporters preferred a comic opera to staying to vote in the Commons—Wilberforce admitted: 'This week I have occasionally felt a sinful anger about the slave-carrying Bill and the scandalous neglect of its friends.' But when, after another failure seven years later, the Clerk of the Commons said kindly that, with his experience in life, Wilberforce really should not expect to pass such a measure, Wilberforce replied, 'I do expect to carry it; and to carry it speedily.' His faith was resilient because it was not in himself, but in 'God who has given the very small increase there has been and must give all if there is to be more'.

It needed to be, for the assaults on him amounted to character assassination. While he was yet a bachelor, it was authoritatively rumoured that he was a wife-beater—and that this non-existent wife was a Negress. Others called him a Jacobin—a term equal to 'Nazi' during World War II. 'If anything (ie rioting) happens to our island, I should certainly, if I were a planter, insist on Mr Wilberforce being punished capitally,' said Lady Malmesbury in 1791.

How did Wilberforce maintain his poise in the face of such attacks?

Undoubtedly he was armoured against them by his first decision. His journal makes it clear that his week-long struggle in November 1784 whether or not to visit Newton centred around his willingness to be identified with the keenest, and so the most spoken against, Christian force of his age. This rising politician and established social success wanted to be better, but not to be thought odd. But he won his battle, for on 12 January he wrote: 'Expect to hear myself now universally given out a methodist: may God grant it may be said with truth.' After that, although temptation returned, it was vanquished. 'Blessed be to God for the day of rest and religious occupation wherein earthly things assume their true size. Ambition is stunted...' he wrote in 1805 when tempted by the offer of cabinet position. To understand the magnitude of his victory over himself one needs to remember, with Trevelyan, that Wilberforce 'could probably have been Pitt's successor as Prime Minister if he had preferred party to mankind'.

So the battle, private and political, raged on. In 1804, a Bill was passed in the Commons, but four royal Dukes took their seats in the Lords to vote it down. In 1806, however, the abolitionists hit on the argument that it was against the national interest to strengthen France's West Indian economy by delivering them slaves. So two thirds of the Trade was stopped, and this made possible the final abolition victory one February night in 1807.

'Well,' said Wilberforce back home that night, 'what do we abolish next?' The answer was slavery itself, and by the strange symmetry which seemed to govern his life, this too was accomplished. As he lay on his death bed, Wilberforce heard that Parliament had voted £20 million so that the eight hundred thousand slaves in British territories could be freed within a year.

This, of course, was not a one-man job. The instrument of change was a band of like-minded men—six Members of Parliament, a former Governor-General of India, a director of the East India Company, several publicists and clergy—who centred round the village of Clapham. 'No Prime Minister,' commented one historian, 'had such a cabinet as Wilberforce could summon to his assistance.' Each had a faith and experience similar to that of Wilberforce himself, and they were backed by the tens of thousands of ordinary people brought to a Christian experience through the Wesleys and the Evangelical movement. These were the foot-soldiers of reform.

The importance of this Christian influence in the abolition of the Trade has, of course, been challenged, notably by Dr Eric Williams, who later became Prime Minister of

Trinidad and Tobago. He wrote in 1961 that their role had been 'seriously exaggerated by men like Sir Reginald Coupland who have sacrificed scholarship to sentimentality and placed faith before reason and evidence'. In particular, Williams argued that during the Napoleonic Wars many traditional supporters of the old system of imperial protection were deserting the West Indian interest, whilst there was an overproduction of British sugar in relation to available markets. In fact, he said, the reason for abolition was purely economic, neither the Trade nor slavery being any longer profitable. This thesis naturally commanded instant assent in interested quarters.

Professor Roger Anstey has since shown in a series of books that Dr Williams' theory is wrong at almost every point. In fact, the Trade was at its most profitable at the time of its abolition and the potential of the slave system was greater after abolition than before. Nor did the overproduction theory hold water. 'The Coupland school was absolutely right,' writes Professor Anstey, 'in stressing that behind the political activity of the religious-minded men who constituted the core of the abolition lobby was a theology of a profoundly dynamic kind and one which... had a profound significance both in the development of a theology of anti-slavery, and for future social reform.'[2]

Other social reform, powered by the same force, followed. It was in the very year that Wilberforce died that the future Lord Shaftesbury took up the fight for the factory workers—a fight which could never have been won while slavery was countenanced. In the next year what might now be called the Tolpuddle Six, all men of faith, began their struggle which dramatised the need for trade unions. Indeed according to Halévy and the Webbs, most of the early trade union pioneers were men of faith and, in due time, Keir Hardie, the founder of the Labour

44

Party, was to say that it was 'the Christianity of Christ which first of all drove me into this movement and which carried me on in it'.[3]

'From the assurance that their sins were forgiven through the Grace of God in the redemptive work of Christ,' writes Dr Anstey of Wilberforce and his friends, 'they knew not only that they could overcome evil in their own hearts but also that they could conquer the evils in the world which they felt called to combat.'[2] So it was with Shaftesbury who, according to the agnostic historians J L and Barbara Hammond, did more than any man or any Government to 'check the raw power of the new industrial system', and with many other great reformers.

Their spirit was that of the Tolpuddle men's favourite hymn which, imitating St Paul, they sang in the stench and chill of Dorchester Gaol:

> All things are possible for him
> That can in Jesu's name believe;
> If nothing is too hard for Thee,
> All things are possible for me.
> The thing impossible *shall* be;
> All things are possible for me.

7

Men can still change conditions

Yes, many people may say, such things could happen in eighteenth and nineteenth century England, but everything is more complicated today. Organisations are so vast and interdependent that individuals cannot initiate significant changes.

Actually, that is not true. Hundreds of people are initiating changes in conditions—large and small—all the time. Here I give three instances from people I have known personally.

The first person is a French industrialist who worked for a fairer world price for a Third World commodity; the second is an Australian Member of Parliament who initiated a new deal for the Aborigines and the third is a young English journalist whose work, according to the Minister concerned, has been largely responsible for ensuring, amongst other things, that twenty-two million British workers now, for the first time, have the right to be told the hazards they face at work.

I do not say that only men of faith could have done what they have done, for courage and concern for others is not a Christian monopoly. But I do say that these particular men would have been unlikely to have engaged in—or carried through—their battles without having undergone the same experience of forgiveness, faith and commitment which Professor Anstey noted in Wilberforce and his friends.

46

Robert Carmichael came from an old industrial family. His Scots ancestors introduced the jute industry into France. At the age of twenty-five he succeeded his grandfather as head of the family business, and within ten years his drive had made him President of the French Textile Employers.

He was known as a just man. As early as 1936, he earned the respect of the Communist head of the textile workers, Maurice Mercier, when he admitted the wages of some workers were scandalously low and initiated reform. But, as a negotiator, he was tough.

Carmichael's family found him tough too. One day in 1946, a young English officer took Sunday lunch with them and, afterwards, suggested that they might spend a few minutes listening to God together. Carmichael, a leading Protestant layman, was not enthusiastic, but his daughter and niece insisted. From those moments a new openness and equality came into the house, and Carmichael began starting each day trying to find God's will.

One of the first thoughts he received was to streamline his activities. So he made a list of all his commitments— the accounts he did for an old lady, the courses he did for reserve officers, even certain of the committees of the Protestant Federation. He went down the list ruthlessly, pruning. He was amazed to find how ready others were to take on the various good works he was led to lay aside. 'There's scope for us, now that Carmichael does not insist on doing everything' seemed to be people's reaction. But Carmichael felt 'quite naked', until he began to see where his unique task lay.

This began to come clear to him at a conference in Switzerland that next summer when he heard some Welsh miners talking to a British employer. They described their sufferings in the depression between the wars and the bitterness they had felt; but also told of their decision no longer to be governed by hatred. They made little impression on the British employer, but they shook Carmichael.

The thought pressed in upon him that he had always put profit before people, and that he had no larger aim than the financial success of his enterprises. He decided, at that point, to put his business life, too, into God's hands.

Where to start? The crazy thought came to him to invite a certain workers' leader in one of his factories, a Communist, to spend three days with him seeing this new spirit at work and to suggest he bring a colleague with him. He was astonished when the man accepted, and brought with him the secretary of the local Communist cell. From that time together came an entirely new understanding. Carmichael brought in better wages—sometimes as much as 50% better—improved housing and guaranteed employment. And to his surprise, he found, after some months that the factory, which had been losing money for years, began to prosper.

In the next years, this same process began to take place in the textile industry as a whole. Mercier, now no longer a Communist but Secretary General of the textile workers in the Force Ouvrière, underwent a revolutionary change at the same conference centre where Carmichael had met the Welsh miners. During the summer of 1951 eighty delegations from the textile industry followed them there, and this facilitated the historic agreement of 9 June 1953. Its spirit was given in the agreement's preamble: 'The textile industry intends to make an economic and social experiment in the interest of the nation, in the spirit of service, with a social objective.'

Practically, this meant that the textile workers were the first in France to benefit from a policy of permanent joint consultation, of compensation for partial unemployment, of bonuses for greater productivity and of mutual, agreed restraint. Every year saw an increase in real wages.

When France was faced with galloping inflation, the Prime Minister turned to the industry and asked them, as the one with the best management-labour relationship, to give a lead. At that time, workers in most industries had forced a 20% rise in wages and, with the consequent rise in prices, were coming back for more. The textile workers responded by accepting an 8% rise and the employers agreed not to increase their prices. Prime Minister Pinay wrote in *Le Figaro* that this agreement was 'one of the first practical realisations of a new way of doing things essential for the economic survival of the country'.

This spirit held through the next decades and led the revival of French industry. During the upheavals of May 1968, following which all the factories of France experienced strikes, some for six or seven weeks, the textile industry was the only one practically untouched.

Meanwhile, Robert Carmichael was concerning himself with an even more complicated problem—how to obtain a fair and stable world price for jute, one which would not only make the European industry function better, but would provide an adequate reward for the producers in India and Pakistan.

Carmichael's concern for the jute workers had begun during an economic mission to Calcutta in 1951. He had come out of his hotel one morning and found himself stepping over the body of a man who had died of malnutrition on the pavement during the night.

That day he had the surprising thought, 'You are responsible for the millions in India and Pakistan who cultivate Jute and who are dying of hunger.' As he returned to Europe he became convinced that the thought was from God and that he must take it seriously.

The partition of the sub-continent, a few years earlier, had left all the jute factories, producing 65% of the world output, in India, but the area where jute was cultivated in Pakistan. Outside India, Europe was Pakistan's only important market, taking half a million tons a year.

As President of the French industry, Carmichael approached the fourteen other countries who imported jute, and meetings in 1954 resulted in the formation of the European Association of Jute Industries of which he was named President.

'The real task of our European industry,' Carmichael told one of the Association's first conferences, 'is to help establish a sound world jute industry. This means giving a fair return to the farmers of India and Pakistan, the right share to middlemen, packers and shippers, a fair return to the processing industries in our own countries and a good product at a satisfactory price to customers all over the world.'

Carmichael had great difficulty in getting this programme accepted. It took much patient explaining—and a few explosions—to get people even to be willing to consider moving beyond personal or national self-interest. Finally, in a stormy meeting in Stockholm in 1959, Carmichael offered to resign. After a day's uncertainty, he was asked to stay on and authorised to talk to the Indians and Pakistanis on his own terms.

Carmichael then made several informal trips to India and Pakistan—the two Bengals—meeting Ministers, exporters and industrialists as well as growers, and speaking generally about the need to stabilise the price of jute. He took with him a film made by the dockers of Rio de Janeiro, *Men of Brazil*, which showed how, as a result of the conversion of rival dockers' leaders, gang warfare had

50

been ended and the first democratic union in the docks had been established. He showed this film to almost everyone he met, particularly when they said his aims were 'impossible' to achieve. 'In particular, I got to know Pakistanis of every background, trade unionists, employers, civil servants, students, Ministers, and entered into their thinking,' Carmichael said later. 'As in Europe, of course, I met intense opposition from some industrialists and from the speculators. But in the course of five years, I was able to bring a certain number of these men to see the necessity for an agreement with Europe and especially with India.'

Meanwhile, trade between the rich and the poor world had been the subject of the first UNCTAD conference in 1964, and in 1965 the FAO succeeded in getting a world agreement on jute prices signed. Unlike other agreements, which had, up to that time, all failed, this agreement only determined targets or guidelines and left the actual price to be fixed each year by a consultative committee.

Six months later, in Rome, the committee met for the first time to fix a price. 'I knew,' Carmichael said, 'that several countries had only signed the original agreement because they were convinced it could not work. The British, I had heard, were opposed in principle. My German colleague had convinced most of our European colleagues that they could not trust the Pakistanis and Indians and had persuaded them to instruct me to do nothing to favour agreement. And meanwhile, in Pakistan, the then President had, under pressure from speculators, replaced the Minister whom I had known, and the Pakistani delegate had instructions to prevent the agreement from working. It looked hopeless. What should I do?'

Carmichael prayed about it. His only thought was to go

a day early to Rome and see the FAO official concerned. During their talk an idea emerged which, next day, overcame the British objections.

Carmichael saw the Pakistani delegate for lunch on the first day. 'I told him my instructions and asked him how they suited his Minister. He exploded, and poured out his resentment and frustration. He felt his own instructions were against the real interests of Pakistan and especially of the jute farmers.'

Then, Carmichael told him his own personal convictions. 'If God allowed the FAO agreement to be signed,' he said, 'we are not meant to fail now. I am sure we can be shown how to proceed in the small pilot meeting this afternoon so that we have a proposal to put before the full committee.'

His own thought, Carmichael continued, was to ask members of the small meeting to leave their official views on one side and to request the Pakistani delegate, the biggest producer and exporter, speaking personally and not as an official, what he really considered to be the fair price in the light of the facts which they all knew.

After a long silence, the Pakistani agreed to co-operate on two conditions—that that part of the meeting should be off the record and that the price he suggested should not be quoted by anyone at the plenary session.

'So it took place,' relates Carmichael. 'And as soon as the Pakistani named his figure, the German delegate said that he was amazed. No one could have imagined that such a thing could have happened and that the Pakistanis should propose so reasonable a figure. On behalf of Germany he would accept it. In a few minutes agreement was reached.'

Next day, the proposal was put to the plenary session and accepted by every country, except Pakistan, whose delegate said that in view of his instructions, he would have to refer back to his Government. He would try to get a reply within five days. He succeeded.

The agreement was applied and brought substantial advantages to the farmers of Pakistan and India. It was the first agreement on a method of fixing a just price for a commodity of which the Third World produced the largest part, and was followed by other agreements.[1] In a sense it was a pioneer effort, forshadowing the break-through at the Seventh Special Session of the UN Assembly in 1975 in which the industrialised West, led by Britain, the EEC and America recognised the need to establish a new economic order of interdependence in which all Third World raw materials would be given fair terms of trade.*

My second example concerns the Australian Member of Parliament, Kim Beazley, whom I first met in 1953 when he came to Britain for the Coronation. A tall, rugged fellow, he had been brought up in poor circumstances, his family much affected by unemployment in the depression of the 'thirties. He won his way by scholarship to the University of Western Australia, where he taught for a time before teaching in a school. After the war, in 1945, he was elected to the Federal Parliament for the Labor Party.

That first time we met he spoke to us a lot about the Aboriginal peoples whose whole culture had been torn apart since the white man came to Australia. They had been driven from tribal lands sacred to them for thousands of years, ravaged by European diseases and undermined by the introduction of alcohol. In Tasmania they had been systematically destroyed, and elsewhere had been

* See page 125

cowed by gun and stock-whip and herded into reserves. Beazley felt deeply for them.

He told us that, while in Europe, he had given his life and his career to God. He had, he said, received the promise that if he did all he could to live a life of complete purity, God would use him to work for the dignity and welfare of the Aboriginal peoples. Purity, he had found, was the answer to living for the self-gratification which kills intelligent caring for others.

Beazley had already, the year before, brought up the question of the Aborigines' land rights in the House. When Captain Cook arrived in Botany Bay in July 1768, his written instructions had been to cultivate a friendship with the Natives and only 'to take possession of convenient situations, with their consent, in the name of the King'. In fact he, and Governor Phillip, twenty years later, declared the whole of Australia to be Crown Land. For two hundred years thereafter the Aborigines possessed virtually no land rights, which was a devastating blow to their dignity and identity, since land was the very centre of their religious concepts.

Through these two hundred years there has been a progressive breaking of hope and spirit among the Aboriginal people. Even in 1868, ten years before the first 'white' test team went to England, an Aboriginal cricket team beat half the first class counties and played the Gentlemen of England at Lords. Today such a team would scarcely be conceivable.

In the long years of Labor Opposition, Beazley began to work for the Aborigines. In 1961 he went to Yirrkala in the extreme North of Arnhemland in connection with the Select Committee on Aboriginal Voting Rights, which resulted in their obtaining the right to vote in Federal elections. There he got to know the Aboriginal leaders.

A little later he returned to Arnhemland because the Yirrkala peoples were afraid of losing all their land which was to be excised from the Arnhemland Aboriginal reserve so that a Swiss company could extract bauxite. Beazley suggested that, since they were now electors, they should petition the House of Representatives, illustrating the petition with their traditional bark painting.

Arising from all this conflict, an enquiry into Aboriginal land rights was made, and during the last five years, their land rights have for the first time been recognised, though not yet adequately.

When Labor came to power in December 1972, Beazley was appointed Minister for Education. During the first Whitlam Government, he carried through an Education Act which the Israeli Ambassador in Canberra described to me in Jerusalem as 'the most creative act of the Administration'. As Minister, too, he at last had a chance to help the Aborigines more directly, initially in the field of education. An early decision was to put every Aboriginal child in secondary school on a virtual scholarship of between $250 and $2,000 a year, and to extend a scheme of assistance at the post-secondary level.

A seminar in the Kimberley area of Western Australia at this time revealed that a majority of Aboriginal children might suffer irreversible brain damage before birth due to malnutrition and disease in their mothers. This was disputed, but the fact that their situation was disastrous was not. This prenatal tragedy is usually compounded by conditions of moderate to severe deprivation before entering school, by which time it is too late for more than a modest 'patching-up' operation to take place. Nearly half the children in one of the better schools were suffering from deafness, lice, scabies, trachoma or a combination of these, and it was found impossible to eradicate such ailments because of the children's home conditions and lack of school facilities and personnel. Such conditions were thought to be typical of other Aboriginal districts, and a leading educationalist described them as 'educational and social disaster areas'.

Beazley was shocked and shamed by these findings. 'For 300 years before European settlement,' he said, 'Indonesian fishermen visited our coast and brought what anthropologists call the Macassar influence to Aboriginal art and language. There is no evidence that Aborigines became alcoholics in a single case because of these contacts, or produced a situation where aboriginal mothers would be so deprived of protein that children are permanently brain damaged. These disasters have come from us.

'I am sorry that I am part of the domination and superiority in this country which always assumes we Europeans know what ought to happen to Aborigines,' he added. 'Most of all, I regret the cruel cutting edge of indifference, the sheer lack of heart involved in our absorption in our own affairs. This leaves Aborigines spiritually, physically and morally injured, treating them as if they were not there or did not matter.'

Beazley set to work to do what he could. In the Northern Territory, which comes under Federal control, he could act directly. Recognising that mission schools, especially those staffed by religious orders, had a commitment to meet the needs of Aboriginal children and their families, and that their teachers might be in the remote areas for ten, fifteen or twenty years learning the Aboriginal languages, culture and customs, the Minister for Aboriginal Affairs, Mr Gordon Bryant, and Mr Beazley put mission school teachers in the Northern Territory on full government school salaries, plus the district living allowances, and met the school costs, releasing mission resources for other services. In the States, where Commonwealth powers in education are not direct, considerable increases in capital and recurrent Commonwealth grants were made. In the Kimberley area of Western Australia finance was provided as a result of a joint meeting of the Federal Ministers for Health, Education, and Aboriginal Affairs to enable the State Government's District Medical Office to recruit able young doctors keen to attack problems of leprosy, yaws, hookworm, trachoma, alcoholism and malnutrition. A strong demand developed for extending this assault by compassionate and committed medical men to other places. That will be an issue for the new Government.

The Kimberley area was under Western Australian jurisdiction, and so it was necessary to work with the State authorities. In one year's budget a sum of $3,014,000 outside of ordinary education, health and welfare appropriations was provided to upgrade Aboriginal conditions there.

It became clear that it was important to use schools for adult education—so that, for instance, Aboriginal parents could use domestic science facilities to learn about nutrition, and the manual arts centres to acquire handyman skills. Schools also needed to be used at night for adult literacy, especially for the quite numerous young Aboriginal men who want to understand motor car manuals!

Beazley believed that to refuse a people who wished it the right to an education in their own language was to treat them as a conquered people. Accordingly the first educational decision of the first Labor Government was that where Aboriginal parents chose, education should be in the Aboriginal languages, and should include Aboriginal art, music, dancing and stories. Aboriginal teachers have accordingly been trained, and teaching material produced. The new coalition Liberal and Country Party Government is maintaining this initiative.

Recognising that only long term planning and co-operation between all departments concerned could reverse the Aborigines' break-down, Prime Minister Whitlam suggested to Beazley conferences of Ministers concerned and a permanent committee of experts to maintain the initiatives. This was approved, and the aim is to make it a bi-partisan Commonwealth and State policy.

'The problem for many Aborigines is that they have caught European values not worth catching,' Beazley says. 'The problem with many of us Australians of European descent is that we transmit values not worth transmitting. We need a real peace between us and the Aboriginal people. Not a peace of successful oppression or unchallenged exploitation, nor a seeming peace, coming from inability to express feelings or a peace of never meeting. We need a peace of straightness of motive, sane expectations, valid aims, gentle intent, freedom from greed, jealousy, resentment, fear and deviousness. The Aborigines have had from us a famine of goodness.'

Beazley's passionate concern for Aboriginal children is based on the belief that each is a 'temple of the Holy Spirit'. 'If you accept the possibility that God can guide men, you are accepting the possibility of a new culture—the culture of the Holy Spirit,' he says. 'Wilberforce's revolution of values (and hence of policy and custom) on the issue of the slave trade and Shaftesbury's on the position of children in the factories were regarded by them as revolutions under the Holy Spirit as their diaries, letters and writings show. We in Australia need a similar shake up of vision in our relationship with the Aboriginal peoples.'

My third instance, the young journalist, happens to be our son, Geoffrey, the Environmental Correspondent of the *Yorkshire Post*. Ever since he first asked God to run his life, at the age of fourteen, he has felt that he was meant to use his pen for forwarding His Kingdom on earth. After university at Oxford, he was lucky enough to get a good job under an editor who, after his initial training, encouraged him to campaign in the environmental field.

His first campaign was to investigate the scandal of Yorkshire's polluted rivers, which were said to be the dirtiest in Europe. In due time, he named twenty-five firms and local authorities as responsible for pollution, and all have since, in some degree, changed their practices. For this investigation he was given two national awards and also the Yorkshire Council of Social Service award for outstanding social service to the county.

In the course of this investigation, Geoffrey ran into a strange difficulty. While any firm which polluted a river or the air could then only be fined £100 for the damage it did, anyone who told the public—or even any other individual—what was coming out of an effluent pipe into a river or a chimney into the air could be liable for three months' imprisonment. This at the time when the then Minister, Mr Peter Walker, was making bold speeches, urging everyone concerned to 'expose the polluters'.

In fact, in order to complete his investigation, Geoffrey had to take water samples from the five Yorkshire rivers at spots above and below each effluent. There was no law against printing this information and saying what effluent pipes were placed in between. So the message got across.

There was a web of legislation, similarly impeding the public's right to know what was being done to them.

For example, under the Factories Act of 1961, a factory inspector was only allowed to tell the management of any unhealthy or dangerous conditions discovered in a factory. If he told anything to a workman, a union official or the Press he risked prosecution, a fine and possibly three months' imprisonment.

When this and other anomalies had been pointed out to the Government, it had replied that the matter would be remedied soon in legislation under preparation. Then, in 1973, reading the small print in a consultative document on the forthcoming Health and Safety at Work Bill, Geoffrey spotted that clauses were proposed which, far from remedying the matter, would increase the penalty on publishing information from three months' imprisonment to two years. After an eleven-day campaign in the *Yorkshire Post*, the paper was told that the proposals would be scrapped.

A series in April 1974 examined the Alkali Inspectorate, and its general policy of refusing to disclose details about pollution from the factories under its control. In the same month Geoffrey's work was featured in a BBC Television documentary. But the insertion of the 'right to know' clauses in the Bill followed a further two-part investigation into an asbestos factory in Hebden Bridge.

The articles showed that 25 people had died of asbestosis or cancer after working at the factory, run by an international company, from 1933-71. About another 150 people who had worked there had developed these diseases. (The latest figures are more than 35 dead and about 200 ill.) Three people who lived near the factory had also contracted asbestosis.

Evidence was given that the company had regularly broken the safety regulations and had never been prosecuted by the Inspectorate. The victims Geoffrey had interviewed said that they had never been warned by the company and some, although vouched for by specialists, had been denied pensions by the Department of Health on the grounds that they had not got the disease.

The articles were read by Mr Max Madden, recently elected MP for the area, who immediately set to work. He sent them to the Minister of Employment, Mr Michael Foot, and Mrs Barbara Castle, Minister of Health and Social Security, asking for reforms. Following a sustained campaign by Mr Madden and other Yorkshire MPs and the *Yorkshire Post* some reforms have been made. Meanwhile, Mr Madden referred the matter to the Ombudsman, who published a report that strongly criticised the Factory Inspectorate's behaviour towards the firm.

Meanwhile, the Health and Safety at Work Bill was redrafted to incorporate the right to know. Not only does it lift the enforced silence imposed upon inspectors, but puts a statutory duty on employers to tell workers about any dangers at work. Management also has to tell people living in the area any hazards they face from pollution, explosions or accidents. Any breaches could lead to two years' imprisonment or an unlimited fine.

These clauses were first announced by the Minister in charge, Mr Harold Walker. He said: 'The section in the act which compels employers to inform staff and the general public about dangers was included largely as a result of the *Yorkshire Post* campaigns.'

Mr Max Madden added, 'The articles certainly caused me to start my campaign. They won important changes in safety law and focused attention at all levels to answer the plight of those working with dangerous materials. The Government's medical checks would have been extended, but on a very limited scale. The publicity extended the checks much further—the distribution of 100,000 leaflets by the Department of Employment obviously happened because of it. Your articles raised important questions about the actions of the Inspectorate and I think they had an effect on the size (tripling) of its increase in numbers and on the fact that it is going to be much tougher.'

Dr Bertram Mann, a leading expert on asbestos diseases, says: 'The saga of the campaign over asbestosis at Hebden Bridge has been the most socially rewarding of my medical experience. There is not the slightest doubt that large numbers of lives will be saved as a result.'

They were being generous. Dr Mann, with others, had already been pressing for an inquiry into the tragedy at Hebden Bridge. And—once he had learned about the situation through the articles—Mr Madden was the spearhead of the campaign. Other media played an important part as well. Geoffrey believes that his articles happened to appear at the right time to act as a catalyst.

These and many other instances have convinced me that people can today, as in the past, alter conditions around them. This is, of course, true whether such people believe in God or not, but the acceptance of God in one's life can be a powerful motivating factor towards such social reform. As the Archbishops have suggested, the first step is often to ask the right questions—and then to take the consequences of one's ideals by changing one's way of living to fit the answers obtained.

8

Those two questions

Dr Coggan's only request to us in his original Call was that we answer for ourselves two questions—what sort of a society we want and what sort of people we would have to become to achieve it.

The temptation, of course, is to treat this like an examination paper where only one question need be attempted. The trendy, politics-is-all clergy tend only to answer question number one and ghetto-type Christians cosily confine themselves to question two. In fact, if anything real is to be achieved, both questions must be attempted.

A friend of mine, Sydney Cook, and I found ourselves forced into this very position some four years ago when our daughters, Angela and Mary, challenged us to take on with them the job of putting on paper our conception of the Christian revolution. They had been stimulated by the appearance of *The Little Red School Book*, which, while seeming to be a book of avuncular advice to school children, was (according to one of its original Danish authors) something very different. So we wrote *The Black and White Book*[1] which, to our astonishment, has already appeared in twenty-two languages and sold over half a million copies.

One of the first things we had to do was to set down what kind of a world we wanted to come into being. And this—since the book was to be written for the kind of people who would naturally read *The Little Red School Book*—had to be done in plain, non-theological terms. All four of us, we found, believed that the Lord's Prayer is more revolutionary than the Communist Manifesto; that the highest aim of man is to do what we can to make 'Thy Will be done on earth as in heaven'. We wrote:

'We want to see a world where everyone has work, food and a home; where a man's character matters, not his colour; where industry aims to answer the needs of humanity, and is not an endless battle for control, profit and wages. Where no man or woman is exploited—or worshipped; where rich nations help and respect developing ones, and big nations do not bully small ones; where Communist and non-Communist countries face what they have done wrong and take on together the shaping of a just society.'

An unrealistic vision? Perhaps, but no more unrealistic than the Lord's Prayer or the Sermon on the Mount. 'Christianity,' Dr Ramsey, when Archbishop, told students at the London School of Economics, 'is the most revolutionary creed in the world because it seeks a revolution in man.'[2]

So what kind of a person must we aim to become if that kind of revolution can take place? What is the true revolutionary personality like? Of this we wrote:

'The true revolutionary is passionate for what needs to be done and not deterred by what people say can not be done. He is not run by fear or flattery and is trusted because he tells the truth. He sees others as they could be and helps them to be their best: hates wrong, but not wrong-doers. He rejects the relative standards of morality by which men justify what they know to be wrong. He is for absolute standards that will cut like a laser beam through the rottenness in our civilisation. He has put

64

right everything in his life that he can and is out to put right what is wrong in the world.

'In order to tackle that job, he will not be hooked on drugs, sex or porn—nor on money, power or hate. So he is able to help others to get free to play their part in building a new world.'

It is, of course, one thing to write about such a personality, but quite another thing to begin to become one. In one's own strength, it is impossible. Only the promises of God can give one the courage to start on that road, and only the power of God can enable one to persist: failing often, but committed to seek forgiveness and start again.

But how to know where to start? We started by thinking in terms of absolute, rather than relative, standards. Some people say that absolute standards are useless because they can never be reached. That, we found, is their value. They are like the North Star. No ship has ever reached that star, but seamen check where they are and where they need to head by reference to it.

Without an objective reference point it is so easy to compare ourselves with others, giving ourselves the benefit of many a doubt, and to conclude that we are as good as, or better than, most. Then one does not change at all. Jesus told His disciples to 'be perfect even as your Father in heaven is perfect', and the passage which the command sums up leaves no doubt at what degrees of purity, honesty, love and unselfishness He wished us to aim. Salvation, of course, must come through faith, and Jesus so often said, 'Your faith has made you whole.' But, in what has become one of the least quoted sentences in the New Testament, He told the woman He refused to condemn, 'Sin no more',[3] and the need for us to put right what we have done wrong, when it is within our power to do so, comes through at many points.[4]

65

So Angela and Sydney Cook, Mary and I, took the standards of absolute honesty, purity, unselfishness and love—a rough and challenging summary of the Sermon on the Mount—and examined what needed to go out of our lives and what needed to come in, if we were to attempt to become Christian revolutionaries. Each of us asked God to show us where to begin. There were relationships to put right, secondary motives to discard, unrevolutionary aims and habits to leave behind. If 'Thy Will be done on earth as in heaven' is accepted as a commitment rather than repeated as a pious drone or a casual insincerity, it is a commitment which brooks no rivals.

A great Christian put it this way to a young man who wanted to work with him:

'If you are going to work around here, you please start living by the Cross and not by rules. You know what that means? Well, we will discuss it together.

'Do you trust the God you serve? Feel He is absolutely reliable? Absolutely reliable? You have got to get to the place where you prefer Him above all men and things.

' "Lovest thou me more than these?" He said that. Can you answer "Yes"?

'My boy, that is where you have to get to. Without Him, don't cross the threshold. With Him, travel the world. It is true: "He walks with me and He talks with me and He tells me I am His own." You ever have that sense? You should. It's your birthright.

'I advise you: make absolute honesty your policy. Don't think avoiding sin is the goal of life. Some do, and a damn dull job they make of it. You have got to have a true sense of direction in which you go all out. Do you have it? What is your speed? If you are moving fast, the dirt does not stick. Same with sin.

66

'Are you smothered with miracles? You ought to be. They are not rationed, you know.

'Your heart has got to come alive. I do not feel a heartbeat in you. You need a blood transfusion. Plasma. "The blood of Jesus Christ His Son cleanses us from all sin." It is life-giving stuff.

'He gave blood, pints of it, for you, to restore you to life. Do you let Him lead? What does lead you? You have got to get to the place where you prefer Him above all men and things. Shed every secondary motive.

' "Make and keep me pure within." Pure within. No heart is pure that is not passionate.'[5]

On another occasion, this man added: 'The Cross is not a real Cross if it is only something on a hill two thousand years ago. It is an awful and devastating contact with the Holiness of God, which breaks but remakes, which condemns but cures, which hates the sin but loves the best in us, which shatters but makes whole, which is the end, but also the beginning, and which leads to the death of self and to the newness and the power of the Resurrection life of Jesus Christ.'[6]

Since it was largely through this man that Cook and I—and so our daughters—became Christians we put his first experience of conversion in *The Black and White Book*. And, strangely enough, as well as asking ourselves much the same questions as those contained in the Archbishops' Call, we ended with a section headed, like theirs, 'Over to You'. The encouraging thing is not so much that the little book was taken up in so many languages, often by people whom we had never met, but that we have received hundreds of reports of practical Christian action which readers of it have taken. That is why I so strongly believe that anyone who asks himself, and tries honestly to answer, the Archbishops' two questions—and then takes the consequences of such answers—will be surprised, as we have been, at the result. He will have put his feet on an adventurous path.

When the talking has to stop

The Archbishops concluded their Pastoral Letter with the words, 'These topics call for study, group discussion and prayer, leading to action.' So they clearly intended that a time would come when the talking had to stop and action would begin. Indeed, a Call which starts from the premise that the nation is 'drifting into chaos' must expect fairly immediate action, if it is to be taken seriously by the public at large.

What kind of action is expected? Dr Blanch, in his forthright address to the General Synod, says that Archbishops can take initiatives but that leadership will have to come from the Church as a whole. 'I see it,' he said, 'in three ways:

'1. From Christians who carry into their secular life convictions about the nature of the Kingdom of God and the rule of Christ which they will seek to apply with subtlety and with rigour in the establishments to which they belong.

'2. From local churches alert to the needs of the local community...

'3. From the national Church, through the institutions which are peculiar to it—Bishops in the House of Lords, General Synod, its Boards and Councils.'

'For far too long,' he added, with special reference presumably to point three, 'we have been simply reacting to national and world events, speaking when it is too late to influence the course of events, protesting when the moment of decision has long since passed, following dimly in the trail of dynamic and very often not very convincing minority movements, and climbing on to bandwagons at just the point where they are grinding to a halt.

'But we have, after all, our own objective which is prescribed to us and that is the "Kingdom of God"—the rule of God in human affairs.... We ought to be bringing it to bear upon the life of the nation in positive rather than simply defensive ways. The best form of defence has always been attack.'[1]

Such honesty and vigour is refreshing. But how is it to be done? What, above all, is the plain individual's part? Many, probably most, of the tens of thousands of people who welcomed the Archbishops' emphasis that 'every man and woman counts' are now finding it very hard to discover what they can do, other than discuss matters in groups which again do not know what to do as a group except discuss. That way lies frustration and, it could be, disillusionment, a far greater danger to the Archbishops' initiative than the most virulent opposition could ever be.

So how can the individual or the group discover what they uniquely can do? The Archbishops' original wish was that the step after study would be 'group discussion and prayer, leading to action'. What kind of prayer, individually or in groups, can lead to action?

My own prayer—and much of the prayer with others in church or elsewhere which I have attended—has so often nothing to do with action, except action which I expect of God. 'Please send me this and let it be nice and come quickly'—just like someone speaking to a tradesman on the telephone, not waiting for an answer.

Then someone told me about two-way prayer—that

70

God could speak to men as well as hear them. 'When man listens, God speaks. When men obey God acts. When men change, nations change.'

Let's be frank. Neither the Archbishops, nor the Prime Minister, have the power to direct the kind of insurrection of ordinary people which is needed if the nation is to be saved. It will take millions of choices by millions of people every day. There is only one intelligence who could direct such an operation and who is in direct touch with everyone, everywhere, simultaneously—God, speaking with the still small voice in every heart. And every group, for 'when two or three are gathered together in My name, there am I in the midst of them'.[2]

The Bishop of Lincoln, the Rt Rev Simon Phipps, has followed up the Call by putting three questions of his own. They are '1. In what ways does God speak to us? 2. How do we listen? 3. What do we hear Him saying? 'What is needed,' he added, 'is that Christians should learn to listen to God so as to pick up His signals with the antennae He has given us.'[3]

How does it happen? Pope Paul told us how not long ago.

'There are two basic ways to learn, understand and possess the Divine Word,' he said. 'The first could be defined as external listening—scholastic, catechistic or cultural. It means learning what the Lord has said.

'There is another way of listening, to listen to our inmost self. This gives a predominant place to the relationship between God and man.... Do you hear the voice of God which inspires, orders, counsels, directs and consoles—the true promise and hope of destiny that awaits us?

'It is not an easy matter.... There are a thousand other voices around us. We are in the midst of deafening noise.

Newspapers, television... how can we distinguish the voice of the Lord which is not more resonant than the rest? The Lord, in fact, does speak in grave and solemn terms, but His voice is mild and gentle. He speaks to those who want to listen.

'He who does what he likes—listening to temptation, instinct, gain and self-interest—is treading a false path. We must, on the contrary, listen to the voice of God with its authority, with its mysterious preponderance over all human voices, even the inner ones... the desires, of the heart must come after the absolute primacy of the conversation with God.'[4]

Dr Coggan himself has written: 'Prayer in question form is prayer in one of the best forms, for prayer is seeking after God, His nature and His will. This is dialogue—the asking of questions, and the listening for an answer. The child, ignorant and groping, seeks the Mind of the Father. This is the reverse of the child dictating to the Father—which is a travesty of prayer. The man who prays is content to ask questions—"Who...?" "What...?"—and is not impatient if the answer is delayed or if it comes but slowly and partially. "Here we see through a glass, darkly..." but as we continue to ask questions, persistently and humbly, we shall be allowed to see more, here a little, there a little, and one day "face to face".'

This passage comes from Dr Coggan's reflection upon the conversion of St Paul. The reflection concludes, 'There followed the second question-prayer: "Lord, what am I to do? What do you want me to do?" At once, the will sprang into action. "I was not disobedient to the heavenly vision," he was later to tell King Agrippa. Christology alone could conceivably remain simply a theological exercise—but not when the question "Who art Thou,

72

Lord?" was asked in earnest prayer, as was the case with Saul. The person of Christ, the obedience of the will—these pregnant question-prayers were not left unanswered —"Get up and go into the city, and you will be told what you have to do." A step at a time. Stop praying. Act.'[5]

There is, as Dr Coggan infers, nothing new about 'two-way' or listening prayer. It occurs many times in the Acts of the Apostles, and generally resulted in detailed instructions.[6] When the men in the Acts obeyed, far-reaching changes in people and events resulted. The saints—St Augustine, St Francis de Sales, St Teresa of Avila and a host of others—speak of it. In our own day, Alexander Solzhenitsyn writes of 'that still internal voice which previously amid the surfeit and the vanity used to be stifled in the roar outside'[7] as sustaining and directing many in the Gulag Archipelago and Laurens van der Post relates how detailed prompting saved many lives in a brutal wartime prison camp.[8]

It is, I am sure, no accident that these men of our time found that art of listening, in times of danger and privation, when they were at the end of their wisdom, and the pride and self-sufficiency was stripped away. Dr Coggan says much the same when he speaks of 'a child, ignorant and groping, seeking the mind of his Father'. There is a lot of evidence that so-called primitive peoples know more about 'listening' than most of us, perhaps because their 'antennae' have not been atrophied, as we have allowed ours to be. Children, too, find it most natural.

The saints won their way back to that simplicity, but there is no reason why we should not do so. They were very practical. St Francis de Sales said that half an hour's listening each day is a basic minimum, except when you are very busy. Then a full hour is necessary.[9] St Augustine[10] and Père Gratry insist that you write the thoughts down. 'God does not stop talking any more than the sun stops shining,' wrote Gratry. 'When shall we listen? In the morning before the distractions and activity of the busy day. How? You write it down. Write it down so that you may preserve the Spirit in you and keep His words.'[11]

A plain suggestion of how one can begin the practice of listening prayer was once given to me by a distinguished scientist, then the Executive Secretary of the American Academy of Sciences. 'Guidance operates in my life,' he said, 'when I do four things:

'1. Listen. Take time to listen first thing every day. Take time enough to forget time. Seek the deepest thought and conviction in your heart.

'2. Write down my thoughts. Then I capture each one and can be free for the next one. Some are not worth capturing, but some are.

'3. Test them—by absolute standards. Is the thought absolutely honest? pure? unselfish? loving? We have known since childhood that these standards are right. They make a reliable check point.

'4. Obey. If I have a thought that meets the test, I need to follow it. Do what God says, not what I want. If I am uncertain, I can talk it over and listen with others who try to live under God's guidance.'

Such prayer inevitably leads on to action. Much of the rest of this book consists of examples of how ordinary people, people I know myself, have taken such action in today's world—and especially in today's Britain.

10

People's action

Evidence that ordinary people can find what each can uniquely contribute was given at a remarkable meeting in the Royal Festival Hall on 4 June 1975, at about the time when the Archbishops were considering their Call. It showed that people of all kinds are willing to change their attitudes and this can have a significant effect on their milieu.

The meeting originated in two events, seemingly unrelated to each other, which happened at about the same time in different parts of the country to people who had never heard of each other.

One morning in May 1974 a Kensington housewife, Mrs Lydia Granby woke with the idea that she should take the Royal Festival Hall for a day in 1975, International Women's Year, so that the ordinary women—not leaders or politicians—could meet and consider the future. The only day available was 4 June. She booked it, but had not by February 1975 found anyone to help her use it. So she gave the Hall back.

Three days later she had a strong feeling that she should take the Hall back again—and soon after she came across a Housewives' Declaration* which had been written by two farmers' wives in Herefordshire. She got in touch with them and, just five weeks before 4 June, they agreed to take on the day with her. It looked an impossible

*See page 83

proposition. All the organisations Mrs Granby had approached had told her that such a gathering would take two years to prepare.

The farmers' wives, sisters-in-law called Erica and Kristin Evans, had written the Declaration under a sense of conviction similar to Mrs Granby's. 'We wanted to take part in building a just society,' said Erica Evans, 'we were fed up with the constant appeals to self-interest and the assumption that housewives were only concerned with their own standard of living. We felt ordinary women could do something and wanted to invite everyone to start with us.'

They printed a thousand copies of the Declaration. It caught on, and 30,000 more were needed in a few months. Other countries were interested. It even reached M Jean Rey, the former President of the EEC. 'This is fantastic,' he said. 'We in Brussels say that things with you are not decided by Parliament but by the British housewife. We need this in Europe.'

So, on 4 June, the two strands came together, and 2,100 people gathered for the day in the Festival Hall. Speakers ranged from the previous year's President of the National Council of Women to the National Secretary of the Salvation Army Home League, from a gold medallist Branch Chairman of the National Union of Dyers, Bleachers and Textile Workers to a British Davis Cup winner, from the President of the Bangladesh Women's Association in Great Britain to the daughter of a former Cabinet Minister in South Africa's Transkei.

There were speakers from both sides of the class war barricades, over which fewer and fewer minds meet. Betty Gray, a former teacher from Newcastle, said: 'We in the seventies are prisoners of the unhealed bitterness of the thirties.' She told how, at the age of fourteen she had been

76

in charge of the family while her father was away seeking work and her mother was ill. 'My mother got worse, but I didn't dare call our doctor because our last bill from him was unpaid. I could not send for my father because he would have great difficulty in finding the fare to come home. So I waited. Then mother became delirious, and I had to call the doctor. He walked up the garden path, very angry, complaining that I had called him at 7 am when a previous bill was unpaid. Half an hour later my mother was dead. You can imagine the depth of bitterness in our family. We saw other people living in affluence, at times flaunting it, and it seemed to us that they did not care how people like us had to live. Many of us developed a passion to have a bigger and bigger slice of the national cake when the opportunity presented itself.'

As she grew up, it seemed to Mrs Gray that Britain was being operated for the advantage of the moneyed class only. 'In our bitterness we decided the day would come when we would wrest it from them and make it belong to us alone, even if the country had to be brought to its knees first. This is what is happening in Britain now.'

She had herself come to see that bitterness is a killer destroying the people who hold it and often other people who have no part in its cause, and when she decided not to be ruled by it, to stop justifying it and let it go, she at last found a meaningful faith in God. 'I found I could lay all bitterness at the Cross—and that it could be healed. This freed me to take work alongside anybody who wanted to take part in a more radical revolution which is for people of all classes, beliefs and colours.'

Nancy Hore-Ruthven, a playwright and actress, said she was brought up at exactly the opposite end of society. 'We had a lovely home in the country with twelve bedrooms and five acres of garden, and we took this privilege entirely for granted.' About twenty years ago her father, a retired Colonel in the Black Watch, mother and all the family took a hard look at themselves and decided they wanted to live to make a society where the kind of thing which had happened to Mrs Gray as a child would not happen to others. They sold their house and voluntarily took on a much lower standard of living in order to make resources available for projects of social value to the country.

'Today we have in Britain great affluence and great bitterness,' continued Miss Hore-Ruthven. 'I want to shoulder the selfishness of my kind of person and my class—the indifference and sheer determination to hang on to everything we have got, which has created the situation we have got today. I want to launch a movement not just of restraint, but of change and sacrifice from the "top". We cannot ask our great trade unions, many of whom have members like the Gray family, to exercise restraint in wage claims if we, who have not suffered that kind of background, do not.

'We need a movement of millions of people who are ready to start with themselves and are ready, in a very un-English way, to tell why they are doing it,' concluded Miss Hore-Ruthven.

Mrs Kristin Evans said their aim in writing the House-wives' Declaration was to set the values of the nation right. 'We take for granted the things that people in most parts of the world would give anything for—food, health and education.'

We had to get our sense of values sorted out, she said, and this depended on our passion to see that everyone had enough to eat. 'We know how much our children pay for their chocolate,' she said. 'Do we think whether the children of the West African cocoa growers are fed?'

Various families said what different clauses in the Declaration had stimulated them to do. It had challenged Mrs Maisie Croft, a grandmother of seven, living in a small Edwardian House in Sheffield, to 'care about the standard of living and true happiness of families across the world'. Starting with the conviction that a cup of rice should go from every Sheffield home to the starving in Bangladesh, she set out along her street armed with a kitchen cup, a large plastic bag and copies of the Declaration. After four months and hundreds of visits, she had collected two tons of rice worth £700, which she and those she enlisted had packed in eighteen tea chests, six drums and six sacks and had managed to get shipped free by a Bangladesh shipping line. Now it was being distributed to the poor by the Bangladesh Girl Guides, and standing with her in the Festival Hall was the leader of the Bangladesh women in Britain.

'I have never worried about anything like this before,' said Mrs Croft. 'But now I am very passionate about the people in the Third World who have not enough to eat while we, although we grumble, are very well off.' Her action had been widely publicised in Sheffield and many people had got involved. A race relations officer had said it was the greatest thing that had happened for racial relations in the area.

A South London housewife, Marie Embleton, illustrated the Declaration sentence: 'We will make new friends including people of different backgrounds and races.' She had got to know various immigrant families whose children went to school with her daughter, but it would have ended there but for an unusual experience. 'Two years ago,' she said, 'I had reached the end of the road. I was living the wrong way and was deeply troubled in spirit.' A West Indian cricketer, Conrad Hunte, visited her family one day and suddenly asked her, 'Marie, would you like to have peace of heart?' She had been resisting every approach from God and man, but she found herself saying openly, 'Yes. Very much indeed.'

'Let's listen to God,' Hunte had said. They did—Hunte, her husband and she herself.

'In those few moments I felt the presence of Christ in that room,' said Mrs Embleton. 'I knew that I was forgiven, cured and free. The next day, waiting in our car in a traffic jam, the thought came to me that I must write a play portraying the experience of the day before, and the plot came floating into my mind. I wrote for three days, and *Britain 2000*, a play about two families, one English the other West Indian, was finished! I had never written a play before.'

Now the play itself has been performed by an inter-racial cast—Indian, African, West Indian and English—drawn from her neighbourhood, in many of the cities where racial problems are most severe. 'Wherever we have gone, Community Relations Officers, the police, Councillors and Members of Parliament have said it has made their work easier. And a force of people has emerged, people of different colours and cultures who otherwise would never have met. We are working together to find God's design for our country.'

An Irish couple from Belfast spoke together. To them, the clause in the Declaration which had struck home was: 'We will refuse to let entrenched attitudes of the past shape our future.' Jim McIlwaine, a senior shop steward in a 100% Protestant factory, said it had led him to travel in a party with a Catholic priest to America with the idea of giving American leaders a truer picture of Ireland and how they could really help. When he and the priest were in the same room Jim would go to the other side of it. Then

God put the thought into his mind, 'Jimmy, you're a fraud because you have said in the past that the Catholic people in Ireland didn't want to be part of the government of your people, but in your heart you've despised their culture and you've used that as an excuse to justify much of the discrimination and bigotry that went on in your country.'

He had been a Christian for twenty years but for the first time he had faced the deep prejudice in his life and apologised to the priest. 'We have learned to respect each other—and that is what we need more of in Ireland,' he said.

His wife, Mary, said that some Protestants had decided to boycott Catholic shops in her neighbourhood. She had been tempted to change from her hairdresser to a Protestant one. But she had known that this was wrong and had gone back to her original one.

'Then when more violence happened where we lived, a lot of Catholic people decided to move out. My hairdresser said to them, 'No, I won't move. These people have given me their custom. So therefore I'll stay with them.' And a lot of these neighbours who had practised discrimination have come back to my hairdresser to get their hair done. One lady said to me that it was the people at our part of the road that actually saved the whole neighbourhood because, had we given in to prejudice, everyone would have had to leave the road.'

Dr Frances McAll, a GP married to a psychiatrist, said that all over the country doctors were trying to tackle, with tranquillisers, sleeping pills and whatever advice they were equipped to give, the tragedy of men and women who are ill because of stress in their personal lives. There were married couples facing the alternative of break down or break up; girls weeping over the thought of bearing a child and facing the deeply disturbing alternative of having to destroy it; women with the alternative of being worn out with the strain of running a home at the same time as doing a full-time job or of doing without some of the things which we have come to regard as essential. What was the way out of such situations?'

'Fortunately for us,' continued Dr McAll, 'the Great Physician is permanently on call. There is no waiting list and no one has to wait for an appointment. I have seen people who have accepted His diagnosis and have followed His advice triumph over insurmountable difficulties. Impossible relationships have become possible, divorce and abortions have proved unnecessary, and unwanted children have become wanted.'

The most constructive thing which she and her husband had done for their six children and their patients had been the giving of the first hour of each day to turn to God, letting Him speak to them about themselves, Himself and the people they needed to help.

'There is absolutely no need for hells, domestic or national,' she concluded. 'But don't let's be like the small boy who once said to me, "I'm too ill to take my medicine. I'll take it when I'm better." '

Since the Festival Hall meeting, its initiators have heard of Housewives' Declarations, modelled on theirs, which are having wide effects in Australia, New Zealand, Malta, South Africa and Canada. A letter from Auckland says, 'We are already on our second 10,000, and are just beginning. It is being used by mayors and mayoresses and church leaders, put up in hospitals, hostels and libraries and commented upon on radio and in the Press.' Cassettes of the meeting are also stimulating many. 'The first evening I told our women about the cup of rice for Bangladesh,' writes Miss Saidie Patterson, the Chairman of the Northern Ireland inter-community movement, 'Women Together', 'I collected £20 for three families whose fathers had been murdered coming home from work.'

'As the letters come in,' says Mrs Erica Evans, 'it reminds me of that sentence in the Queen's Christmas message: "The smallest pebble thrown into a pool will change the whole pattern of the water." '

NOTE

HOUSEWIVES' DECLARATION

We are grateful that most of us in Britain have enough to eat and to keep us warm and to those whose work makes this possible.

We will tackle today's difficulties as a challenge and not depress others with our grumbling.

We will care about the standard of living and true happiness of families across the world. Have we the right to get richer every year when so many are hungry?

We accept that food will cost more everywhere. We are ready to spend less on luxuries. We will shop from need and not from greed or for hoarding and will re-think how much is enough for us.

We will refuse to let the hurts and bitterness or entrenched attitudes of the past shape our future. We will accept honestly our own share of the blame for our present troubles.

We will make new friends, including people of different backgrounds and races. We will put right disagreements with old friends and neighbours starting from our side.

We will think for ourselves about what is right and be ready to stand firm and speak out for it.

We will take on the building of a different world for our children and grandchildren. We know this cannot begin without a change of basic human motives which needs the power of God. It will mean the moral re-armament of our country to free it from greed, hate and fear. We will start with change in ourselves and in our homes.

11

'Enemies at our gates'?

No part of Dr Coggan's original Call led to more impassioned argument than his plea for 'strong, happy, disciplined homes'. The TV screen leapt to life as parents bashed the matter to and fro, and one father seemed to object to all three adjectives.

Dr Coggan returned to the subject in his New Year message. Our hearts, he said, should go out in compassion to those whose homes were broken, but we should not pity those who, by teaching or example, undermined the foundation of home life.

'I think,' he continued, 'of parents whose example leads young people to think that marriage vows do not matter, of teachers who manipulate rather than educate, of theorists who would lower the age of consent, of blind leaders of the blind who shut their eyes to inconvenient facts such as the fact that 95% of Borstal inmates come from broken homes. Such people as I have mentioned are the enemies at the gates of our society.'[1]

Some would say that people who lend themselves to one or other of these activities are already well established inside. For example, it was Dr John Robinson, the former Bishop of Woolwich, as Chairman of the Sexual Law Reform Society, who presided over the Press Conference when the Society's working party advocated, amongst other things, the reduction of the age of consent for girls and boys to fourteen and the legalisation of incest for people over fourteen.[2] And now Mr Jenkins has appointed a Policy Advisory Committee, with the age of consent as the first point on its agenda. Mr Ronald Butt, *The Times* columnist, finds little public demand for such changes and says the only explanation he can suggest for Mr Jenkins' decision is 'a willingness to heed the pressure groups campaigning in these fields'. Prominent among these is the Paedophile Information Exchange, defined by Mr Butt as 'the lobby of the child-molesters now euphemistically called paedophiles', which complains: 'Society makes it almost impossible for our relationship to exist.... We are warm and gentle people. What has to change is attitudes to children's sexuality and parents' attitudes to their children.'[3]

Does this whole process mean that Dr Robinson and Mr Jenkins could be among 'the enemies at society's gates'? Not, certainly, in general—or by their intention. Dr Robinson is a man of wide sympathies and great learning, whose virtues need no defence from me. Mr Jenkins is one of those rare politicians who has shown himself ready to risk his career, again and again, for his convictions. Indeed, for what little that is worth, I often find myself in agreement with each of them. If, however, the kind of legislation publicised by Dr Robinson were enacted—say, by a private members bill with Mr Jenkins' active help—it would not be the first time such a thing had happened. There was, for example, legislation making divorce easier, abortion and homosexual practice more acceptable and the display of almost any obscenity in print or on the stage possible. Bishop Robinson spoke of such reforms as 'a necessary step towards the mature society'[4] and Mr Jenkins hailed them as the coming of a 'civilised society'.

Each of them has laid down his underlying philosophy

quite clearly. The Bishop, for example, states that he does not like abortion, but that 'love has no interest in keeping people moral by Act of Parliament'.[5] One understands Dr Coggan's choice of the word 'theorists' when one realises that the millionth recorded abortion under the 1967 Act has now been reached.

Mr Jenkins, too, produces unexceptional theory. In his celebrated speech of 19 July 1969, he explained that he regards the 'permissive society' as a misnomer. 'A better phrase,' he thinks, 'is the civilised society, a society based on the belief that different individuals will wish to make different decisions about their patterns of behaviour and that, provided these do not restrict the freedom of others, they should be allowed to do so.'[6]

An admirable theory. One does not doubt Mr Jenkins' theoretical ability or his sincerity. It is his innocence and inconsistency which are so alarming.

He seems so innocent of knowing how human nature works and what the results of his legislation are likely to be, in the absence of the public adopting, at the same time, a very much higher moral standard to guard themselves, their children and the nation from excess. Actually, as could have been foreseen, the standard declined, partly as a result of the legislation he encouraged. This has made the results of the legislation even worse than was expected.

Mr Jenkins might have been warned by the unforeseen results of the Tory-backed Gaming, Betting and Lotteries Act 1960. This Bill was presented as 'the clergyman's charter' under the illusion that all it really did was to permit lotteries for good causes and one of its sponsors went so far as to suggest that 'some of the lure and attraction of gambling will disappear when it becomes legal'. The actual result was that, within six years, there were five thousand gaming-clubs in Britain, excluding

Bingo clubs, and the gambling turnover had risen to over a quarter of the national budget.[7]

Mr Jenkins' inconsistency is equally strange. He obviously believes that laws do encourage the creation of a new moral climate, for that was the raison d'etre of his important legislation against racial discrimination which relies principally on persuasion rather than prosecution.

Then, why should he think that the loosening of moral laws would lead to 'the civilised society' rather than to a flood of anti-social self-indulgence? Does he now foresee the disastrous results of the lowering of the age of consent—the widespread exploitation of unformed girls and boys—or is he once more lost in a haze of theory?

His inconsistency was all the more remarkable in view of the fact that, by the time he made his 'permissive is civilised' speech, he had migrated from the Home Office to the Treasury. It was wedged between other speeches in which he exhorted us to be more disciplined, to work harder, and to be more moderate in our demands for financial satisfaction. Why should self-indulgent people become disciplined and public-spirited when they put on their coats and go out to work? Why should those who think it civilised to deceive their wives and get away with an easy divorce resist breaking a contract? Why should we confine our instant gratification to the sexual sphere and forswear it in economic matters which fuel inflation?

Mr Butt mentioned the influence of the permissive lobby, the hard core of which was once described by Mr Kingsley Amis as those who bought unexamined the abortion-divorce-homosexuality-censorship-marijuana package—the key words being 'unexamined' and 'package',[8] since there are obviously thoughtful people who could have serious reasons for championing legal reforms associated with one or other of these words. The hard core are those who, as Miss Pamela Hansford Johnson once remarked, react to any suggestion that pornography might be dangerous 'with unthinking tantrums, the tantrums of a child clutching to its breast some precious, grubby toy rabbit it cannot bear to part with.'[9]

Miss Hansford Johnson ran into this kind of permissive storm-trooper during her investigation of the Moors Murder in which a girl aged ten and two boys aged twelve and seventeen were murdered in particularly bestial circumstances by people who had soaked themselves in the literature of sadism and torture. The natural question after such a case was whether some measure of censorship might be desirable or whether at least authors and publishers should practise some self-restraint lest they encourage the harming of other innocent children—a point of view which, by the way, has since been reinforced by other cases. Miss Hansford Johnson could find 'very few intellectuals indeed who would lend themselves to any serious discussion' of the question but that 'any attempt to get them to discuss it responsibly and without exaggeration often drives them into a strange sense of hysteria... or to total silence'.[10]

Miss Katharine Whitehorn, *The Observer* columnist who states that she 'generally votes the straight progressive ticket', has noted something approaching the same hysteria in the talk about divorce. 'I cannot help feeling it odd,' she wrote, 'that divorce is talked of in enlightened circles as if it were a benefit that should be made available to all, rather than a tragedy it is worth almost anything to avoid.' Divorce was increasingly spoken of as a 'relief', 'as if the only possible picture of marriage was of two people gagged and bound together by the ties of Church and State'.[11]

The danger is that words like divorce, abortion and censorship—and other words are always being added—have become emotive to the extent that the permissive pioneer reacts with the predictability of Pavlov's conditioned dogs. A new orthodoxy has been created, a 'sleeping up with the Joneses ethos', to quote Miss Whitehorn again, which, in certain circles, 'puts the faithful and the virgin, if any, badly on the defensive'. 'In the age of freedom,' she continues, 'it is "that rarest of the sexual perversions, chastity", that is least readily allowed.'[12]

Meanwhile, the *Observer Colour Magazine* devoted almost an entire issue to an enquiry entitled 'Are We the Last Married Generation?', in which contributors maintained that 'marriage is too demanding and crippling' and the editors wrote that it 'is now being eyed for its possible unsuitability to human nature'.[13] And when two Conservative Ministers in the Heath Government resigned after being involved with prostitutes, the Greater London Young Conservatives suggested that special safe, state brothels should be maintained for the use of Cabinet Ministers and visiting politicians.[14]

Lord Kilmuir, the late Lord Chancellor, once remarked, 'We are rapidly drifting into the situation that the obvious way of avoiding sin by not committing it is thought to be too difficult for mankind.'

One is vividly reminded of this dictum when one reads some British comments on the recent Vatican declaration 'On certain questions concerning sexual ethics'. 'It's cruel of the Pope to make such statements,' said a social worker, 'a lapsed Catholic living with her boyfriend'.[15] 'This is going to torture very excellent Catholics with a sense of guilt,' declared a psychiatrist, Dr Elizabeth Tylden. 'Premarital sex is a matter of fact and thousands of couples will now find themselves in a state of sin. Normal sex behaviour is terribly important.'[16] 'There are a number of minority groups,' added the Chairman of the Catholic Renewal Movement, Mrs Ann Hamlyn, 'who do suffer greatly in their consciences because of the Church's very rigid teachings.'[17] 'It makes sinners of us all and that makes it a nonsense,' concluded Dr Michael Smith, until recently medical adviser to the Family Planning Association,[18] in words providing an up-side-down image of the General Confession. One would think Pope Paul had invented Christian ethics specially to spite them.

Indeed, it is now clear that many people have far outpaced Lord Kilmuir's observation and now maintain that sin is not only inevitable, but outstanding virtue and, indeed, a cure to our condition. Ingmar Bergman recently maintained that one of his films had increased the divorce rate in Denmark and 'that's got to be good',[19] and a medical witness in the *Inside Linda Lovelace* case argued that pornography of extreme cruelty should be available to all because he would prescribe it for some patients.[20]

I wonder sometimes whether Mr Jenkins is quite so sure these days that his Obscene Publications Act of 1959 was the first bright dawn of 'the civilised society'. Its preamble, once more, stated excellent theoretical aims— 'to provide for the protection of literature and to strengthen the law concerning pornography'. It was swiftly shown not to be strong enough and so a further Act in 1964 was brought in 'to strengthen the law preventing the publication of matter for gain of obscene material'. The Linda Lovelace case shows how completely the objects of both Acts have been destroyed by the perfectly legal exploitation of the Acts themselves.

Mr Norman St John-Stevas, who drafted the original Bill which led to the passing of the 1959 Act, seems to be having second thoughts. He says a 'change in the law is now overdue' and blames the 'unsatisfactoriness' of the Act on the growth of permissiveness. 'It presupposed a widely accepted public consensus of what constitutes depravity and immorality which can be acted upon by a jury. The existence of such a consensus could be presumed in the 1950s, but the permissive revolution, for good or ill, changed all that.'[21] What Mr St John-Stevas does not, as far as I am aware, ever admit is that he has unconsciously encouraged the very tendencies he now deplores.

It is possible that the Linda Lovelace case may awaken people to the danger of unbridled permissiveness—and to the uses that permissive pioneers and their allies, the commercial exploiters of sex and violence, make of woolly-headed and poorly drafted legislation. Perhaps, too, the Attorney General may reflect on his refusal to call expert witnesses in view of the quite opposite decision in a parallel case when a private individual, following the Crown's refusal to act, brought Dr John Court, from Australia to give what turned out to be decisive evidence.[22]

Certainly, there is very little sign that the majority of the British people want the present state of affairs to continue. Similarly there is little support, except in a narrow group of 'enlightened' intellectuals, for the idea that the family is finished. In a recent poll 94% of the British people thought 'the family structure of supreme importance' and 77% stated that 'marriage is essential'.[23] The contrary view is only held by a noisy minority. 'Journalists and sociologists have agreed for years that the extended family is dead and the nuclear one liable to fission,' writes Miss Whitehorn. 'Then we suddenly read that three quarters of the nineteen-year-olds and 42% of old age pensioners live with their families. It makes one wonder if we're talking about the same country.'[24]

12
Families matter

Most people, then, agree with Dr Coggan that the family matters and that it is worth working hard to build, protect and provide for. The main question is how this can be done. For a lot of us seem to find it very difficult.

There were over a million divorces in America last year, while half a million children ran away from home. In Britain the number of divorce petitions per hundred thousand of the population has tripled in the last ten years and exactly the same has happened in Russia.

American sociologists give various explanations for this situation. A hot favourite is the 'destruction of the extended family'. 'All sorts of roles now have to be played by the husband and wife whereas in the older family they had all sorts of help, psychological support, financial advice and so on,' says Dr John Platt of the University of Michigan.[1]

Cornell sociologist Andrew Hacker says, 'The problem is summed up in one word—women.' 'Until recently,' he says, 'wives were simply supplementary to their husbands and not expected to be full human beings.... The institution we call marriage can't hold two full human beings—it was only designed for one and a half.'

The Yale psychiatrist Kenneth Kenniston, on the other hand, spotlights 'youth', 'a new stage in life which did not exist in earlier centuries'. Millions of young people now remain outside the work force and go to college, thus making possible today's separate youth culture. Remaining in this milieu often till their late twenties, 'they are still questioning family tradition, family destiny, family fate, family culture and family curse.' This, he says, unsettles the families from which they spring.

British pundits also have their theories. Some think modern marriage just goes on too long. 'An average couple,' writes Professor Northcote Parkinson in *Mrs Parkinson's Law*, which he assures us is not autobiographical, 'may have enough in common to enjoy perhaps two years of each other's society. By the third year they may suspect that the opposite of Polygamy is Monotony.'

Dr Edmund Leach, the Provost of King's College, Cambridge, in his Reith Lectures, was even more sweeping. 'With its narrow privacy and tawdry secrets,' he said, 'the family is the source of all our discontents.' He went on to suggest that 'something like the Israeli kibbutz or the Chinese commune' would be a better bet.[2]

Each of these institutions was a response to national needs at a certain point in time, and neither seems very appropriate for export. Chaim Bernant writes that 'the kibbutz today is, in fact, a large family full of small families screaming to get out.' 'Even if the traditional family is not the most efficient—or even the most wholesome—social unit, it is the most natural one,' he adds. 'Alternatives could be devised—the kibbutz is one of them—but, given time, there will always be a reversion to the type of family traditionally known. The family will out.'[3] And the Kibbutz, which has obviously done the Israeli nation great service, only includes 3% of the Jewish population anyway.

The average Chinese commune, on the other hand, is said to consist of some forty thousand people, and Western apologists for them insist that the ordinary family flourishes within them. Experimental communes have sprung up all over the Western world in imitation, but one authority writes: 'To survive, communes must be authoritarian, and if it is authoritarian it offers no more freedom than conventional society. Those communes based on freedom inevitably fail, usually in one year.'[4] 'Some religious ideal,' concludes Patrick O'Donovan, 'has always been and probably still is the most powerful mortar for building a commune.'[5]

So Dr Leach's alternatives do not seem universally applicable. And even if they were, we would be little further on. For the same problems arise in them as in the traditional family. Such families are going to continue to be the most natural basic unit for most of mankind, so we had better set about finding what can make them work better, while remembering that many millions work well already.

The truth is, of course, that families experience every conflict which exists in society. They have sit-ins, go-slows, and stay-outs. They know violence and sabotage, cold wars and wars that are not so cold.

Indeed, family crises sometimes seem harder to solve than larger ones. Labour and Management generally know that, whatever their present tensions, they must one day work together again. Warring nations will still be neighbours after hostilities have ceased. But husband and wife can part for good—or at least for ever—and young people can walk out never to return.

All this, together with current statistical trends, could seem pretty hopeless if there were no power known to man which can alter people's characters and heal raw relationships. But Christians know that such a power does exist, and will, if we are willing, work with amazing speed and accuracy. So family problems, even the toughest, can be solved.

I, for one, have seen dozens of divorces averted and hundreds of dreary marriages become fresh and bright again. I have also seen young people freed from drug addiction, and parents freed from no less deadly addictions to comfort, booze or their own way which drove their children to despair. I can also say that I have not known a single marriage which was begun on the basis outlined in chapter nine—where both parties honestly sought the direction of God, examined their motives and consulted wise friends—which has broken up, and I have known many hundreds in all kinds of countries and circumstances.

Many marriages, of course, get off to a bad start because the motives for getting into them were inadequate, or just wrong. Others break up later, through boredom or tension. The causes of misunderstanding are as varied as human beings themselves, and it is impossible in a few pages to outline universal solutions. Yet there are certain things which we have found essential in our own quite imperfect family and which many other families, too, have found helpful. At the risk of superficiality, I give them below.

First, we believe that every family needs a purpose. The last thing to aim at is a 'happy family', for happiness only comes as a by-product. The important thing is to have an aim in common, so that each of us can see our own desires, plans, triumphs and disappointments in a wider perspective.

Our family aim is for a just society, where His Kingdom comes on earth as in heaven. When we are all working for this, all out together, many smaller disagreements never take place and others are more easily resolved. And having this kind of purpose means, incidentally, that there is no chance of ever becoming an 'isolated nuclear family'. The family naturally expands to include hundreds of friends of every class and kind.

Secondly, we find that the generation gap is generally an honesty gap—beginning with us parents. A father in a re-united family said to me the other day: 'I said my son never communicated with me, but then I never communicated with him.' The son was there, and something new had obviously happened. It had started when the father said: 'I have realised there is only one problem in this family—and that is me.'

I never found my children responded to lectures—or parental wisdom from a height. 'May I go now, Dad?' our son once said to me when he was young and I tried it on. But if I was honest about myself, my failures at his age *and* at that moment, as well as my hopes, then he quickly responded. Our relationship still rests on that basis now that he is in his late twenties.

Quite a few children these days say: 'Why should I try to get on with my parents? I did not choose them. Far better to leave them alone and get on with friends whom I choose for myself.'

Our daughter answered such a suggestion: 'I've just been in Southern Africa trying to help resolve a racial situation justly without bloodshed. To do that, you have to work with all sorts of people you would not choose.' That is so if you want to get anything straightened out in the world. And if you can't do it at home, why should it work elsewhere?

Actually, trying to get on with a few friends whom you have chosen does not always work so well either. Such relationships often get sticky and sugary, and then, by reaction, spiteful.

Thirdly, we find that our family needs a boss, but no human being is fit to be it. I, the father, certainly am not. Sometimes the father runs a family, sometimes the mother and often the children. In days past there was much talk of deprived children—and plenty still exist. But now there are many deprived parents—fathers and mothers who dare not cross their children's wills because they are terrified of losing their love. Really, being soft and fearful like that is the quickest way of doing it.

Children feel quite different when they know that God has been asked to be head of the family, and all—parents and children—are equally people under authority. Then when we listen together, we are all equal and all respect each other as God's children.

Fourthly, families need to know how to resolve difficulties. Of course, it is much easier when you have a common aim—an aim, that is, which is imposed by no one but freely undertaken by all parties—but even then difficulties arise. This is where the impartial reference to God is so essential. Apology to God and each other is a healing experience. We need forgiveness every day.

An important thing is to keep short accounts—not to allow a criticism or a bitterness or a hurt to fester, but quickly to get it into the fresh air together.

When we practise these precepts—and not just talk of them—we find we are a united family, whether we are living near together or continents apart, and we become effective to help others. When we don't, the generation gap soon reappears. Through the years it has been when we parents have settled down to middle-aged comfort and indulgence that the children have got bored or disillusioned.*

* Anyone wishing to know how it has worked out in the ups and downs of our family life will find details in *Good God, It Works!*

The curing of broken or breaking families can come from either end, as is shown by the true stories of two Scandinavian friends of ours both named Anton.

Anton Pedersen is a handsome young Dane who used to be the lead singer in his own pop group and part of the local drug scene. He quit home at fourteen when his father, who was bringing up five children on a twenty acre farm, took him out of school without consulting him.

Anton was top of his class and dreaming of university. His father set little store on book-learning. He told Anton to find a job and pay his own way. Anton got a job on another farm, and hated his father for it. He would show him.

Next year, Anton won a scholarship to one of Denmark's local boarding schools. From there he went on to a pre-university course in Odense, working for his living all day in a glass-house, doing his homework in the late afternoon and attending school at night. At weekends he sang with his pop group which soon began to get commercial bookings. Secretly his parents were proud of his progress, though he was bitterly divided from them. Sometimes he went home for an hour or two, but got away as soon as he could. 'I resented my father, and found less and less in common with him and mother. I despised their lack of education. I found we just could not communicate.'

Meanwhile at college, the state of the world was impinging upon Anton, and he began to wonder whether all his hard work was worthwhile. 'Our discussions of world problems left me hopeless,' he says. 'There seemed nothing an individual could do to change them, and soon the only thing left seemed to be to opt out of society. I did this by taking drugs. I just thought I would have as much fun as

99

possible and that I wouldn't care a damn about anyone, or even whether I lived or died.'

One of his friends did die, for his crowd which had started by smoking pot moved on to LSD and some to heroin. Two of them suddenly took off for India with their state education grants in their pockets. The news that one of them had died there of drug poisoning came in the same week that Anton was expelled from his course for drug taking and idleness. By now he had also left his job at the glass-house. He had come to a full-stop. He did not tell his parents, but lay low with a family from whom he rented a room.

Just then this family was driving on holiday to Switzerland and they offered Anton a seat in their car. They wanted to visit their daughter who was working at Caux, the same international conference centre visited by Robert Carmichael.* In his ten days there, Anton was deeply affected.

'It was the first time I had met people who had a positive programme on an international scale for putting things right,' he says. 'And they said I could have a part. Amazingly, they cared enough for me as a person to challenge me to change and to believe that it could happen. I decided to have a go. It was a 180 degree change and it was painful, I can tell you. But I quit drugs then. That's seven years ago, and I have not touched them since.'

On his return to Denmark, Anton sold his share in the band in order to pay Kr 2000 of undeclared tax on his past earnings. He was also honest with his parents, telling them about his expulsion from college. He did not find it easy. Some time later he also apologised for his superior attitude towards them. 'Immediately I apologised, my

*See page 47

100

bitterness disappeared. I suddenly saw that they had a lot of wisdom and experience from which I could learn.'

'That healing helped me to keep my decision to live a different life,' Anton says. 'All my friends who had taken to drugs or got into trouble had one thing in common—they all came from broken or bitter homes.'

Anton hitch-hiked back to Caux. He had been invited to take part in a musical show which young Europeans were taking to Asia. It was called *Anything to Declare?* and its theme was what helpful things Europe had from its experience to say to the people and governments of Asian countries.

Anton felt that this trip would give him a chance to see if his new friends' global effort really worked, and he saw clearly that the challenge came home to him personally. What had he himself to give?

About this time, he started to get up earlier in the morning and to give the first half hour of the day to God. He was not very sure that it was God speaking to him—or who had helped him over the drugs. But he tested each thought by Christ's standards of absolute honesty, purity, unselfishness and love—and if the thought passed, he followed it.

One thought he received was to give up smoking tobacco. This he found as hard as giving up drugs. 'I took out a final cigarette, and enjoyed it, knowing it was the last. Then I threw the rest away.' It was a struggle, but in his need of help for that struggle God began to become real.

But the event which sealed Anton's faith in God happened in India the following Easter. He went to the church on Easter Day, and suddenly a desperate realisation of guilt for the way he had treated his parents and friends swept in on him. It was an intolerable burden. 'In that moment I turned to Christ unreservedly, and I shall never forget the sense of forgiveness which flooded in. He had died so that my sins might be forgiven. I decided that I would accept it and live for Him.'

One of the places he visited with *Anything to Declare?* was Papua New Guinea, a country which is taking a great leap from the stone age straight into the twentieth century. For many this means, as one Papuan leader states, 'crossing ten thousand years in a lifetime'. A part of this process has been the achievement of political independence.

Seldom can there have been so many obstacles to nationhood. A thousand tribes speaking seven hundred different languages live in this vast country. They are kept apart by impenetrable jungles, crocodile-infested swamps and mountain ranges which sometimes rise to over four thousand metres. Tribal wars and head-hunting were till quite recently the rule for many, and the country's great mineral wealth, typified by the world's largest open-cast copper mine at Bougainville, makes the transition even more abrupt.

Facing this situation, the leaders of the new country were searching for new ideas to form the basis of a workable national philosophy. Some of them who had heard of the all-African film *Freedom* which had helped Kenya through its first elections without bloodshed. So they translated it into Pidgin, the local language, and invited a team of young men from several countries to take it through the land. Anton was one of them.

This entailed travelling thousands of miles by aeroplane and dug-out canoe, on foot and by jeep. It meant fording flooded rivers, getting stuck in bogs and falling into creeks. And there were stiff climbs to the Highlands villages where they slept in kunai grass huts and lived on

102

the local diet of 'kaukau'—Pidgin for sweet potato—with meals only once or twice a day.

Anton found that it was his personal experience—of freedom from drugs and smoking, of reconciliation with parents and of knowledge of the difference between good and evil, of Christ's forgiveness—which helped him in Papua New Guinea. Tribesmen in their grass huts immediately knew the difference between the good spirit and the bad spirit which warred inside them. They caught faith from Anton and his friends.

One of Anton's Papua New Guinean friends was some time ago attending a youth conference in Manchester which was visited by a leading British cabinet minister. The minister discovered where he came from and remarked:

'Ah, Papua New Guinea. You have a lot of tribal problems there.'

'Yes,' replied Anton's friend, 'but we have great hope in that four of our new cabinet members give time to listen to God each morning.' Then he added: 'It seems to me you have a few tribal troubles yourself in Northern Ireland. I don't think they will be solved without God's guidance.'

'You may be right,' the minister replied.

So far Papua New Guinea has achieved independence in peace, and its leaders say that men like Anton have made a real contribution.

Back in Denmark, Anton found that his father had got discouraged with farming and that he had sold his cattle and was working in an iron foundry, just cultivating a single cash crop on his land in his spare time. The foundry did not agree with him and he fell ill.

It was at this time that Anton was able to tell his parents more fully of his sorrow for the way he had treated them. 'We felt much closer together,' explains Anton, 'but it was hard to know whether I was doing any good because my father is a reticent man. However, it would seem that about this time he decided farming was the right job for him after all and he set to with new confidence. It has worked out. Today he has thirty cows and all the family are doing well.'

Another Anton who came at the family problem from the opposite end is Professor Anton Skulberg, the Norwegian MP and biochemist. He, like Anton Pedersen, went to that same Swiss centre in some perplexity. He was worried to death about his younger son who was doing badly at school. This son had reluctantly come with him.

'I was haunted by fears for him, fears of narcotics and school failure,' says Professor Skulberg. 'I was so afraid that I started to put him under control. It began with encouragement, developed into nagging and then became pushing. He lied to avoid my control, and was easily found out. Then fear gripped me and I imagined all kinds of things. When you are frightened—and grossly ambitious for your children—you don't use your head or your heart.'

Lying in bed one morning, the Professor suddenly remembered that his own father had once tried to control him and how he resented it. In the same moment, he saw that it was his fears which were the root of the problems—and which might well drive his son to the very courses he feared for him. 'I asked God what to do and knew that I must apologise for my nagging and pushing. But how? I was not sure my son would listen.'

The Professor decided to write his son a letter—and to write in French, a language in which he was not fluent enough to be slick. 'I felt God must give me every single word.' He put the letter on his son's bed.

Two days later he found a reply on his own bed. Then they were able to begin talking again. A friendship grew between them. The boy started to do better at school because he now knew he alone was responsible.

'I learnt that if you want responsible people, you have to give them responsibility,' concludes Professor Skulberg. 'This was a very important preparation for me, for two months later I was appointed Minister for Education and Church Affairs. I would never have been able to do that job if God had not released me from my fear and created a new situation in my family.'

The first thing which Dr Skulberg did after his appointment was to call in the Press and tell them that the absolute moral standards of Christ were now fundamental for him.

'The most important thing when you are a Minister is to make decisions,' he now says, 'and it happens too often that decisions are taken under the influence of fear. In such a job the guidance of God is vital. The fields one is expected to cover are so wide that one cannot possibly know every detail. When one considers that one's decisions will have an effect on every individual in the country, one is grateful to share the responsibility with Almighty God.'[6]

So the change in each of the Antons has influenced the lives of thousands. And it is true, again and again, that a remade family can have a wide effect, perhaps just because God has had to work such a visible 'miracle' that others are given hope.

Genis Ibot is a twenty-year-old Filipino of slight build and quick-silver intelligence who comes from the island of Mindanao, where a civil war between Christians and Muslims has been raging for the last fifteen years. His family has been involved in it, because his mother is a Muslim while his father has been a Christian army officer, as are his brothers. Their house was destroyed in the fighting and two of Genis' Muslim uncles were tortured and killed. As a result his parents broke up and Genis, at sixteen, intensely bitter at his father's ill-treatment of his mother, fled to a Muslim refugee camp where he was taught to use arms and explosives against the government forces.

To this camp came some Christians who were so humble about their community's mistakes that it made Ibot think. 'They did not mention anything about their particular religion, but one of them told me about the "inner voice"—and that everyone has the free will to choose either for good or for evil. I tried it, and became convinced that real change can only come through radical change in people's hearts and motives, and not from the barrel of a gun.'

One of the first thoughts Genis received was to find his parents and apologise to each of them, especially to his father. He also returned to him a gun and some bullets which he had stolen from him and used against his father's people. 'It took a miracle to make me honest about my mistakes and not just blame them for theirs,' Genis says. 'This honesty brought reconciliation to my family. It took many weeks, but now my parents are together again. My father apologised for his arrogance and irresponsibility. My mother had wanted to take revenge against him. But she forgave him and they were reunited.'

The leader of a camp of Muslim guerillas in the mountains heard of this reconciliation and asked Genis' mother to come to their stronghold and tell them about it. She accepted and took her husband, a retired army officer, with her. It meant risking their lives, but their direction from God was to take no gun or other weapon with them.

'When they arrived at the rebel hideout, 140 rebels were waiting for them,' Genis continues. 'My parents spent six days and nights with them discussing what had happened to our family and challenging them to face the change in the heart needed to bring order to our country. They also discussed together the dangers of other ideologies using the minority problem to invade the Philippines. The mother of a Muslim leader said to my mother: "Five years in the jungle running away from bombs and machine-guns had planted bitterness in the hearts of our people. But after hearing from you we feel that we are healed."

'On the fourth day my father went down to the city to invite the military officer in charge of the area to come to the mountain camp. The officer accepted. Together with the Muslim rebels they worked out an agreement based on a change of heart and the inspiration of the inner voice.'

On the sixth day the officer, Genis' parents and some of the rebels went down to the city of Cotahato where a conference was to take place between Muslims and Christians. The Governor of the island of Mindanao, the Commissioner and representatives from the Government, the Ambassador from Saudi Arabia (some Arab countries have been involved in attempts to resolve this conflict), and leaders of both groups were there.

At the conference Genis' mother was asked to take the agreement they had worked out in the jungle and present it to the Acting Vice-President of the Philippines in Manila.

On 6 June 1975 she presented the agreement and it has since been ratified. It guarantees the rights of the Moslem people and the unity between Muslims and Christians, but also includes provision of food, housing materials, medical aid, farming equipment through loans and the rebuilding of schools and mosques.

'This agreement covers only our province. But many people in Mindanao have seen this miracle and have been given the challenge of a new alternative they could try,' says Genis. 'I am very grateful that the Almighty has chosen to use our family for this work. This miracle gives me real hope that a personal change can lead to social changes.'[7]

The fact is, then, that desperate family situations can be solved, and that remade families are a factor of tremendous potential in larger situations. If a Danish pop star, a Norwegian Cabinet Minister and a young Muslim guerilla can be so effectively reached, and the change in them can have such far-reaching influence, what could not the two million British Christians, to whom Dr Blanch has referred, achieve in our disunited country and beyond? But we may first have to ask ourselves whether we are willing to learn to become 'life-changers' and to take the consequences, in our own lives and families, of allowing God to equip us for such a task.

It will call certainly for a new quality of family living. For when Dr Edmund Leach said that the family is 'the cause of all our discontents' he may, in a way he did not perhaps intend, have been more right than we care to admit. I have hardly ever known a really bitter man whose bitterness did not start, often quite early, in his home. Equally, there are few children who have been deserted by one or other parent who are not deeply affected. The problem is not so much that illegitimacy is socially unacceptable as that the child feels rejected. And many, even when they have been well cared for by foster parents or those who have adopted them, carry a chip on their shoulders all their lives. A recent BMA report states that the death of a parent is far less damaging to a child than is a break up by divorce.[8]

It is the failure of family life, through our selfishness, wrong aims or just plain ignorance which is the cause of the discontent, and not, as Dr Leach inferred, the institution of the family itself. That is still meant to be—and still is, in the majority of cases—the power house of joy and the cradle of character for mankind.

13
'Work matters'

'Good work matters,' said Dr Coggan at his press conference. 'A good day's work for a fair day's pay isn't a bad motto for worker and management. "Each for himself and the Devil take the hindmost" makes for chaos.'

One of the interesting questions which will no doubt be answered in *Dear Archbishop...* is how this and other parts of the Call have been received by management and workers, and particularly by the workers. For, rightly or wrongly, they are not only regarded as being the key to national survival, but are also the sector of the community where the Church is said to have least foothold. The Bishop of Liverpool, David Sheppard, says that when he was Bishop of Woolwich, he reckoned that a middle class suburb-dweller was ten times as likely to be a churchgoer as was a worker. So it will be fascinating to know what proportion of the letters arriving at Lambeth and York came from trade unionists and what such letters said.

The public response of trade unionists so far has been meagre. Predictably, the *Morning Star* characterised the whole Call as 'union-bashing', but there is no reason to believe that the mass of trade unionists felt this. The factory workers appearing on *Anno Domini* with Dr Coggan were non-committal rather than hostile, and Mr Basnett was mildly encouraging.

My own soundings have produced some more positive reactions.

A worker from London Airport, a long-time shop steward, had encountered the *Morning Star* line on the Call. Referring to the Archbishop's words quoted at the beginning of the chapter, he said, 'Well, what's wrong with that? He's only repeating what the Government and some trade union leaders have been saying. In fact, he went one better when he included management in his motto for industry. Previous exhortations have always been slanted towards trade unionists.'

A life-long left-winger, Albert Ingram of Birmingham, was even more encouraging. 'My own reaction,' he said, 'was one of absolute delight, because it allows me to see the Church in a different light. For most of my life I have been contemptuous of formal religion. It has failed to answer problems for so long that I felt it had stopped trying. The Church, I felt, was a form of escapism: an adjunct to life without being any part of essential living. This statement was the first indication to impress me that these people are aware how men like me feel and what our needs are. I want to be convinced that I have been wrong all these years. I shall await developments eagerly.'

But there was a firm consensus among those to whom I talked that the initiative would have to be sustained and more vividly presented if it was to grip the masses. 'It has not become an issue at work,' an inventor working at the Cranfield Institute of Technology told me. 'Those few who have heard about it support it,' said a Boilermakers' official from Harland and Wolff, Belfast. 'But no one is taking any steps as a result. What will count now is action and example.'

I asked some of these men what action an ordinary man could take. One of them is John McKenzie, a Boilermakers' shop steward in Scott Lithgow, Scotland's largest shipbuilders. He told me story after story about the breaking down of demarcation barriers in the yard as a result of the initiatives of various men. A recent story was about differentials.

Traditionally the boilermakers have always been the strongest union in the yards and have set the pace in wage bargaining. Other tradesmen have usually settled for a few pence less per hour. So when the other tradesmen asked for parity, there were voices raised among the boilermakers for keeping the differential undiminished.

When this came up, McKenzie intervened. 'The Boilermakers' Society is based on brotherhood,' he said. 'Brotherhood not only concerns the Scott Lithgow group but trade unionists the world over. We should get away from the old idea that other tradesmen are "jumping on our backs". If we can all agree on the same rise, that is fairer than always sticking to the differential.'

The majority of the stewards agreed with McKenzie. Several thanked him afterwards, and the policy was accepted by a 5-1 majority of the workers. The Managing Director publicly commended it as having been negotiated 'without fuss and fury' and said he was heartened by the realistic attitude of the negotiators that 'industrial survival is everybody's business'.

Whether or not McKenzie's intervention had a major part in the decision, it is significant that he did speak out. 'I always used to be out for No 1, trying to get as much money as possible for as little work as I could get away with. Multiply this and you have Britain's crisis,' he says. 'I used to remain silent at union meetings if I went at all. I was one of the "couldn't-care-less-brigade". Now I speak up—and fight for what seems right for our industry and the country.'

Another example came from a senior shop steward in a large Midlands engineering works who is known as Burglar Bill. Bill is a sheet metal worker who was once arrested, coming out of a pub, by a bobby who mistook his workaday hammers and levers for housebreaking tools. Hence the nickname. Bill told me how he was recently on a twenty-man committee to negotiate a new wage for twenty-four thousand workers. They had been mandated to put claims which would work out as an increase of between £11 and £17 a week. This claim was presented—and both sides retired to consider what should be done in view of the Government's £6 maximum rise. It looked like deadlock.

'I had the thought to give the retiring management and some of our own men a copy of the statement of intent, which some of us had drafted, backing the Prime Minister's idea of "a year for Britain instead of a year for self",' said Bill.* 'To both lots, I said: "In the interval please take a good look at this." We on our side had a long discussion and decided by sixteen votes to four to alter our claim. So we called the management back and said we were ready to negotiate within the framework of the Government's £6. This has now been settled. I can't prove it, but I think that statement had a lot to do with it.'

The former Trotskyite, Albert Ingram, had a good deal to do with drafting that 'statement of intent'. This caused great interest when reported in the *Birmingham Post*[1] because Ingram had been one of a small group who initiated the action which wrecked the Labour Government's attempt to legislate on trade union matters, following Barbara Castle's White Paper, *In Place of Strife*. He was secretary of the Campaign Against Anti-Trade Union Legislation, which was subsequently backed by

* Issued in September 1975 and called 'Action '75'.

113

most trade unions, and the inventor of the slogan 'Kill the Bill' which became that campaign's national watchword.

Now Ingram told the Press, 'I am sorry for my part in that. Now I see what has happened to the nation, and I hope to make up.'

The paper announced that some four hundred trade unionists, many of them Midlands car workers, had united with him in initiating the move. Ingram told me that their grass roots movement was growing and was gaining support in many parts of the country.

When I asked Robert Hansford, the inventor quoted above, what people could do, he talked about the part everyone could play in avoiding wasting our resources. One day three years ago, he had stood at the window of his Buckinghamshire cottage and watched the straw in the neighbouring fields going up in flames after the barley harvest. He thought that there must be some better way of using surplus straw than that.

'Five million tons of it—the equivalent of 2% of our national coal production—is burnt in the fields every year. Most of it goes up into the air, landing on someone else's fields or washing, and doing very little good except leaving a little potash,' he says.

Hansford figured out that the main reason for this national bonfire is that straw is too bulky to transport or store economically. Hauliers are unwilling to use twenty-ton lorries to carry ten tons of straw, for example. Supervised by his colleague at Cranfield, Dr Ian Smith, Hansford found ways of compressing straw bales by two thirds, and a 400-bale per hour press, powered by a tractor, is now being made commercially. 'This machine could become the most important piece of farm equipment since the combine harvester,' comments *The Sunday Times*.[2] The Cranfield team is developing the means for making straw an acceptable, industrial, raw material for livestock feed, plastics and perhaps most significantly as a substitute for imported wood pulp used in the paper industry, so saving hundreds of millions of pounds in foreign exchange while using an excellent home-grown and renewable resource that would otherwise be wasted.

'Each of us,' says Hansford, 'is aware of some waste, whether of manpower, heat or material. We can stop it. But it will take some commitment. 65% of the heat from our power stations goes into the air from our cooling towers. Someone will have to put his life on the line to change that. It may take fifteen years. That is commitment.'

Vickers Oils, the firm mentioned by the Archbishop of York in his address to the General Synod, is headed by John Vickers who is at present Chairman of the British Lubricants Federation. He told me that 'the most important industrial issue is to find a new motive so that we really care for the deepest needs of all men of all kinds.'

'Any dispute can be solved on the basis of *what is right* instead of *who is right*,' he said. 'A revolution comes about when employers really care so that people come before profit—our own firm serves an industry which is still in severe recession, but we have made no one redundant. This is the alternative to the sterility of class war, and is the quickest way to put right what is wrong and to build a new society.

'There are two areas of action. First, inflation. I think of one firm where management proposed, and all the employed staff and workers accepted, an annual increase of income which is two-thirds of the going rate of wage settlements in order to keep prices down.' (His own firm, I happen to know, has several times held prices, against the trend, voluntarily for this purpose.)

'Secondly the leadership which employers can give. For some time I have operated on the basis that whenever there is an important decision, I myself consult with all our staff and employees, in groups as small as possible, so they are informed and can participate.'

A company director in the South of England told me how, just before going to a business appointment, he read a paraphrased version of Psalm 101 where it said, 'Help me to abhor all crooked deals of every kind and to have no part in them.' The man he went to see told him, 'My client wants you to pay the £1,000 you owe him into an account in Jamaica.' The director said he could not do that because it was a tax-dodge. 'A lot of people are doing it,' said the agent. 'How can we expect the miners or anyone else to act unselfishly, if we businessmen are dishonest?' said the director.

All these instances come from people who have, some of them very recently, found a Christian faith. Albert Ingram began to look for something beyond his own mind at the time when his wife died. 'For the first time I needed a faith,' he says. 'More important, I wanted one. A cynical character like me has been proud of his freethinking for so many years. It was a very important step to want, to seek sincerely, to believe in God, and to seek His guidance. It was a total change. I used to preach that hate was so important, because angry people could be more easily motivated the way you wanted. It does not make me less militant. Now, perhaps for the first time, I am really fighting *for* the men at work instead of fighting for myself through them.'

One of those who is doing much to spread this message in the Midlands is a Coventry building worker, Les Dennison, who recently took part in a lively seventy-minute 'phone-in on 'Marxism and Christianity' on

Radio Birmingham's popular 'Morning Call' programme.

'Communists are men who are concerned with what's wrong with society, men who passionately care and believe that Marx had the answer,' he said. 'I long for Christians to have the passion, discipline and world vision of the Marxist. Then you'd find they'd take the offensive and win men such as I was—a Communist for twenty-two years. I met revolutionary Christians who related their faith to what was wrong in society and brought answers—not theories—to society.'

Dennison spoke of his own road to faith, starting with the challenge he received from a Christian—that he fought for the unity of the working class, but he wasn't united in his home. 'Bang, it hit me straight between the eyes. The ABC is reconciliation in the family, new attitudes in industry, and across the world.'

Asked how his fellow workers on the building site reacted to his new ideas, Dennison said, 'I used to tell them what I'd seen; and without exception, the positive, related, Christian experience grips men. You relate your experience of Christ, of God, to the nitty-gritty of the situation you're in in industry, then men listen.'

'So you set out,' asked the compere, 'to show that your Christianity didn't take you out of the fight but it drove you into it with a different kind of enthusiasm?'

'The men I met didn't tell me to stop hating,' answered Dennison. 'They told me to stop hating the men I used to hate, but hate what's wrong. They didn't tell me to stop fighting, they told me how to fight more effectively. So often people equate Christianity with going soft, going easy. I hate the injustices, the exploitation, the degradation just as vehemently as any Marxist, and I fight to put them right.'

I once asked Dennison what had been the decisive

117

moment for him, an intellectual Marxist who did not know what the word 'faith' meant. He told me how he had gone into a church one Sunday early and knelt at the back while a few people were having Communion, not even knowing what they were doing. 'Oh God, I'm in your house,' he said. 'Let's have some evidence.'

He was still there after the service and the vicar approached him. 'What's your trouble?' he said.

'I'm trying to find if God's there,' Dennison replied.

The vicar walked with him to the door, when suddenly there flashed into his mind that a friend had written to him that week about a similar talk he had had with a man in the train between Peterborough and Rugby, a man with an address in his parish. It had been Dennison.

'Let's go and pray,' said the vicar.

The vicar prayed: 'Behold, I stand at the door and knock...'

'At that moment,' says Dennison, 'I was so filled with a sense of my awfulness, of my evil, that I literally cried out for help. Well, I have talked about peace all my life, but I never knew peace till that moment. The simple experience of being forgiven. It was incredible. I came out of that church so different that I thought everyone must be looking at me. I began then to learn the reality of what God can do in a man's life, and it is that faith which has stood by me all these years.'

14

'Attitudes matter'

Dr Coggan quoted the former American Secretary of State, Dean Acheson, to the effect that Britain had lost an Empire and had not found a role. He added, on his own account, that she had not found a soul. Could these two lacks, which few would deny, be interconnected? Could both be due to our allowing our concern to shrink to too paltry or partisan a level?

'Far too many people in the Labour Party,' said a member of the Wilson cabinet recently, 'think that the test of socialism is the release of Des Warren. A much more serious test is what is done about the thousand million poorest people in the world.'

Many Conservatives, it could be added, seem to consider the test of Toryism to be the repealing of the Capital Transfer Tax rather than conserving our planet, Earth, for our children and grandchildren.

The fact is that all parties in Britain think too small and on too short a time scale—and we Christians do the same. That is one reason why we often fail to engage the commitment of the strong spirits of youth. If we are to discover both our national role and soul in the years ahead, the first thing may be for us to cease dwelling in the past and start facing the future, in a global context.

Actually, the whole earth is in a gathering crisis,[1] which will reach everywhere and affect everyone. Major changes will have to be initiated in the next few years, if unnecessary but progressive disaster is to be avoided.

Even the present situation is grim enough. According to the UN Food and Agricultural Organisation, over 460 million people are 'actually starving' at this moment.[2] Meanwhile, the world population will double in the lifetime of most people living today.

At the same time, at least 200 million people in the developing world are unable to get jobs and so are unable to earn a living for their families.[3] 44% of all Indian city families live in one room and there are an estimated 44 million squatters in South America alone,[4] while on a world scale 75,000 people every day are leaving the countryside and pouring into the cities.[5]

Violence, meanwhile, is growing—whether one thinks of street muggings or the proliferation of nuclear arsenals, and terrorists may soon obtain nuclear weapons.[6]

And, on top of all this, there is the environmental crisis. Systems which sustain all life on the planet appear to be reaching the outer limits of their tolerance. 'If we go on as we do now,' wrote the authors of *Only One Earth*, 'then we are heading for ecological disaster.'[7]

From these crises, plus the fear that the world would run out of both food and resources, the doomsters of 1972 concluded the almost inevitable suicide of mankind. In that year, *The Sunday Times* (4 June 1972) reported on a series of computer-runs made at the Massachusetts Institute of Technology.

First, the computer was fed the projection that the world continues as it is, ignoring the problems of overpopulation, food shortage, pollution, running out of raw materials and fuel. Result: imminent collapse from lack of resources.

So, they ran another computer test, assuming this time that a solution had been found to the resources problem.

Result: collapse due to pollution.

So another run assumed control of pollution, too. Result: lack of food causes breakdown.

All right, assume that one is solved and go back for another run. Result: another and even greater pollution-caused breakdown, despite controls.

Surely limitation of the population is the answer then? The computer says, no, not alone. All the five factors have to be controlled at once. Otherwise, however you juggle, it's humanity's suicide.

The method employed to get such forecasts and some of the data on which they were based have now been largely discredited. But they do, at least, illustrate the interdependence of all these crises; and there is no doubt of their basic conclusion that we cannot for long go on along our present course. Since 1972 the United Nations' intensive studies have confirmed that. There are, it now seems, causes common to all these crises, and also potential common solutions. 'Collectively the whole multitude of crises appears to constitute a single global problem of development.'[8]

Take, for example, the population explosion. Much reliance was placed, some years ago, upon vast family planning programmes in countries like India. But they have been disappointing. Now experts generally believe that the answer lies more in a distribution of food than of pills, in wealth control as much as birth control. 'The countries in which population growth has begun to slow significantly are the countries in which the benefits of development have been shared more equally.'[9]

If you think about it, this is natural enough. It is usually the poorest families who have the largest families, because children give them security in illness and old age, help in the fields and joy in lives which often have little of either. So the population crisis seems to be rooted in the unequal distribution of the world's resources.

The first thing which seems to be clear about the 'single problem of development' is that there is no present lack of physical resources. 'There is,' says Sayed Marei, Secretary General of the World Food Conference in 1974, 'no foreseeable prospect of a world food deficit.' Although 460 million people are 'actually starving', enough is, in fact, being produced to feed everyone today, and it is clear that this will be true in 1985 and probably in 2000.[10] The problem is one of distribution, though that is not just a matter of getting food from place to place.

Thus, people in the rich world—the West, the Communist world of East Europe, Japan, etc—eat too much, while the people in the poor world eat too little. If we in the rich world ate only what is good for us, the poor could immediately be fed.

Americans, for example, waste 25% of the food they buy,[11] and another 25% goes not to nourish but to create obesity. A quarter of all Britain's food supplies are also wasted, according to the Chief Scientist of the Ministry of Agriculture, Dr H C Pereira. For example, half of our fish is thrown away. If we were prepared to eat darker fish meat, and bone the fish ourselves, we would have twice as much to eat without landing any more.[12]

Then there is the kind of food we eat. It is estimated that if every American did without one hamburger a week, that would provide enough grain to feed 25 million people.[13] If America cuts its meat consumption by 10%[14]— and the American Heart Association wants a 33% cut to fight off the rise in coronaries—that would give enough to feed 60 million.

Widespread famine was partly averted in the winter of 1974-5 because the recession led people in the rich world to eat less meat and so release grain for the poor world.

Why does a small cut in meat-eating have such an effect? It is because animals today are not just fed on grass, which humans cannot eat, but on grain, milk, groundnuts, soya and fish. And animals make very uneconomical use of these materials. It takes around 7 lbs of grain to produce 1 lb of beef. And more grain is fed to animals in rich countries each year than is consumed by the people of India and China combined.

Restraint—and the sending of grain to the poor countries—is, of course, only a short term solution of famine. In the long term, the answer is to get the poor countries to feed themselves. There is enormous potential in these countries, but they need aid to start the process. The preparatory work for the World Food Conference estimated that aid, to meet this problem, would cost about £2000 million a year for five years—an enormous sum, but in fact exactly equal to the turnover of the British gambling industry or £2 a head per year from every person in the rich countries.

What has been said about food is true of other resources. In general, the fact that the gap between the rich and the poor countries is constantly widening is neither good for the rich nor for the poor. It is, for example, contributing directly to environmental pressures by condemning the poor to cultivate marginal land at great risk of soil erosion or to migrate to the cities, while the artificial cheapness of raw materials encourages waste and the throw-away economies in rich countries. 'While the environmental problems of the industrialised countries stem from their wealth and power,' said Dr Maurice Strong, the first UN Secretary General for the Environment, 'the environmental ills of the developing countries are rooted in poverty.'

The danger of this gap in terms of present and future violence is obvious. 'Morally,' says Willy Brandt, 'it makes no difference whether a man is killed in war or condemned to starve to death by the indifference of others.' 'Can we hope today,' adds Barbara Ward, 'that the protest of the dispossessed will not erupt in conflict?'

For the reasons given above—and because of other factors which cannot be even listed in so short a chapter— it seems brutally clear that there must be a shift of resources, and quickly, from the rich to the poor world. But how can this come to pass?

The poor world is demanding a 'new economic order' and, since the emergence of OPEC as a major force, the rich world seems for the first time to be considering it. For the quadrupling of oil prices did three things—it hit the poor world to such an extent that its need became even more apparent, it shook the rich world into seeing that it could no longer run things entirely its own way and, to many people's surprise, the oil-producing nations have so far, by and large, stood with the poor world and refused to be split from them. Of course, OPEC's money is more liquid, but it is worth recording that at the time when the UN target for official aid was 0.7%, the 'rich world' managed only 0.33% (Britain 0.38%, the US 0.25% and the Communist countries very much less), while OPEC countries gave 1.8% and pledged 5.4%—although it is uncertain how much of this is military aid and there is some doubt where it has gone.

But it is not so much aid as just terms of trade—and help without strings, which preserves their self-respect— for which the nations of the poor world are asking. They do not expect equality or levelling down, but, according to one source, only the means to achieve a basic £200— £250 per head of their population per year.[15] Maurice

124

Strong says that this would not require a cut-back in the rich world, but 'only a percentage of our future growth'.[16]

The UN General Assembly had held two Special Sessions to try to deal with these problems—the Sixth in 1974 and the Seventh in 1975. The Sixth, held immediately after the abrupt escalation of oil prices, was a dismal failure. An empty formula was agreed which all the industrial nations neutralised by tabling formal reservations immediately afterwards.

But in 1975 there was a break-through. And, amazingly, the initiative came in large measure from the British delegation which, immediately after the 1974 debacle, saw that a new initiative was essential and began doing the homework on what would be possible. There was tough opposition in a Whitehall absorbed in Britain's own economic difficulties, but finally the Government, facing a debacle at the Commonwealth Conference if it had nothing positive to suggest, gave these preparations its blessing and backed moves to enlist its European partners and the United States in a radical re-think.

When the Special Session opened in the first days of September, the United States made what has been called 'the most generous speech since General Marshall's declaration at Harvard in 1947'. The Third World, seeing that the West meant business, responded, and Russia and China, who had long posed as the only friends of the undeveloped nations while providing less help than the West and revealing nothing of their own internal positions, found their bluff called and are now having to reconsider their policies. Shortly afterwards, in the Social and Economic Council, the Yugoslav Delegate thanked the British Delegate by name for 'bringing a new spirit in the UN', fulfilling its role of becoming 'a centre for the harmonising of the actions of nations' as defined in the

Charter. Here Britain, in her days of declining power, had been able to be a catalyst for world change. Is it in finding such a role that she may, as a by-product, find her soul?

All the practical details of the agreement are still to be worked out—and will continue to be the subject of negotiation for years ahead. If the plan is to succeed—and all the other looming crises are to be mastered—a world-wide degree of unselfishness and co-operation, which has never been forthcoming before, will be required. Wholly new attitudes will be necessary in rich and poor countries alike—for the inequality within nations is as damaging as between nations—and an unprecedented wave of honesty to back it up.

No statesman or group of statesmen, however far-sighted and courageous can solve these problems for us. Many initiatives, large and small, are needed, but behind them all there will have to be a new level of living in all of us. 'It is no longer a simple moral imperative to demand that everyone should act without rapacity, and respect interdependence,' said Professor Barbara Ward in her keynote to the first UN Conference on the Human Environment at Stockholm. 'It is an accurate scientific description of the means of survival. Today our facts and our morals come together to tell us how we must live.'[17] To which Maurice Strong, the Chairman of that conference, later added that the one hope is 'a moral and spiritual revolution which goes far enough to alter our lifestyles and penetrate our economic and political systems.'[18]

Where are we to get the power to make such tremendous changes? Dr E F Schumacher, the author of *Small is Beautiful*, one of those who have most clearly and practically faced the coming age, asks this very question. 'An ounce of practice is generally worth more than a ton of theory,' he writes. 'It will take many ounces, however, to lay the economic foundations of peace. Where can one find the strength to overcome the violence of greed, envy, hate and lust within oneself? I think Gandhi has given the answer: "There must be a recognition of the existence of the soul apart from the body, and of its permanent nature, and this recognition must amount to a living faith in God".'[19]

Surely we Christians, if we take the Lord's Prayer seriously, have a particular responsibility to re-think our lives in the face of such realities.

Dear Archbishops

Dear Archbishops,

You asked us all for suggestions how your initiative could best be carried forward. Here are mine, which are addressed as much to myself and all other Christians as to you. For we are all on trial together. When the balance sheet of this initiative is made, the test will not be what anyone has said, but how deeply each of us has allowed himself to be changed and how effectively or otherwise we have all worked together to change society.

The change that is needed is something more than personal, something which takes us beyond exhortation, protest or church attendances. It will only affect the nation if it reaches down to our inner motives and spreads out into public policy.

I was struck by something Sir John Lawrence says in his *Take Hold of Change*. 'Every society,' he writes, 'needs some principles of coherence, a religion, an ideology; call it what you will.'[1] Until recently, the word 'ideology' has sent a shudder down most Western spines. This has partly been because the materialist ideologies of Left and Right have left such a bad taste of cruelty and compulsion. But is that the whole story?

As long ago as 1948, Frank Buchman remarked:

'The missing factor in statesmanship today is our lack of an ideology for democracy. We say, we are democrats, we need no ideology. So we try to meet the united plan and passion of alien ideologies with talk and with lip-service to high ideals and with a last resort to force. And we hope to live as we have always lived—selfishly, comfortably and undisturbed. We have all lived too long in an atmosphere of imagining that security, prosperity, comfort and culture are natural to man. We forget the eternal struggle between Evil and Good.'[2]

Is not that very much the same message which Solzhenitsyn has been struggling to bring home to us today, nearly thirty years later?

The fact is that the word 'ideology' is neutral; but it involves a degree of commitment which the word 'religion' has often lost—and from which we shrink. Why should we not live the Christian faith with such fire and thoroughness that it would offer every person in the world an alternative to the materialist ideologies which still, nearly thirty years on from 1948, make the running?

That is certainly what Buchman had in mind. 'We are in a global effort to win the world to our Lord and Saviour, Jesus Christ,' he said on another occasion. 'There is your ideology. It is the whole message of the gospel of our Lord and Saviour Jesus Christ. The message in its entirety is the only last hope that will save the world.'[3]

As Sir John said, we can call it what we will. But, to be adequate, it cannot be lived comfortably, selfishly, respectably, amid the boredom or faint applause of a world whose militant religion is materialism.

So I believe we Christians must, if the nation is to be reborn, face certain realities.

First, we must live our full faith—but keep our vision national, as you did in your original Call. We must put forward our aims in terms which everyone can understand and anyone can immediately apply, however little, much or even lack of faith he may have. We can trust the Holy Spirit to lead not just churchmen, but everyone, into all truth.[4] He is not our monopoly. Our danger now, as through the centuries, is that we fight so strenuously to cut Him down to fit our convenience and narrow understanding.

Second, we must expect the most from each other. People will not respond to less than the fullest challenge, and if they did, it would be ineffective. The present crisis—and still more the hidden crises which loom ahead —demand nothing less than our aiming, in His strength, to be 'perfect'. And that is true whether we believe in God or not.

Of course, we will not manage it—or get anywhere near it. But unless we aim for the best we know, we shall do a lot worse. Hence the value of absolute standards. 'It is a mark of the shallowness of Western life,' wrote Professor William Hocking, 'that it should be thought a conceit to recognise an absolute and a humility to consider all standards relative, when it is precisely the opposite. It is only the absolute that rebukes our pride.'[5]

Why is it that Mother Teresa of Calcutta has such a flood of young people wanting to work with her—far more than she can use? It would seem that holiness is more appealing than trendiness, that chastity is more joyful than what-we-can-get-away-with with a fairly good conscience, that a challenge to the limit brings more hope and satisfaction than being asked to approve of something.

Third, we need to be willing to be seen as we really are. The Bishop of Liverpool and Mrs Sheppard recently told a television audience about themselves—their weaknesses and sorrows as well as their joys and beliefs. At the end of it, thousands upon thousands felt that they had made new friends. How refreshing it would be if every politician, industrialist, trade union leader and churchman was prepared, as occasion arises, to be equally honest. To admit where we have been wrong instead of spotlighting where the other fellow has erred. To acknowledge our fears instead of whistling in the dark. Would not that bridge the gap between politicians and people—and between the Church and the ordinary man?

Fourth, we Christians should heed the wisdom of that great Swedish Archbishop, Nathan Soderblom, who once said: 'One changed life is more eloquent than many sermons.' The time for exhortation is past. But if hundreds upon hundreds of Christians could come forward now, in the factory and the shop, on television and in the Press, and show that a definite change has come into their lives, that would encourage others. Perhaps clergy—even bishops—need now to get others speaking; to stop trying to do ten men's work and to help ten other men to do their work better than they can do it themselves.

More specifically, can the Call long continue—or take fire—if only clergy speak for it? Are there not sportsmen, trade unionists, artists, even Members of Parliament, who could tell of the reappraisal of their lives which they made and of the new commitments they have taken as a result of the Call? Could you not set many such teams on the road? Of course the changes would have to be real and the commitments definite. 'What has happened to whom?' people are asking.

It is in the hope of encouraging people to do this that I have told many stories in this book. All of them come from the lives of people I know personally through a common association with Moral Re-Armament. I do not mention this to claim credit for it, still less to suggest that such evidence is in some way confined within it. Others

131

have access to other treasuries and will, no doubt, bring out of them things new as well as old, for this is a time for everyone to speak up about what he has seen and heard. The battle for national rebirth will not be won by any one church, group, class or party. It will be everyone's victory—or everyone's defeat. Or rather if victory there be, it will be that of God's larger plan working out, through or in spite of us all.

This initiative will provoke opposition. You have experienced a little of this in recent months and you will experience much more if you press your message home. You could receive the modern equivalent of the treatment which your church and mine accorded to John Wesley when he fought his long battle for Britain two centuries ago. That such a reaction is still possible is shown by the hysterical response in some quarters to Solzhenitsyn's sharp, but loving, diagnosis of our state, which prompted *The Times* to ask: 'Are we now a society that welcomes truth or one that prefers the comfortable lie?'[6]

Opposition is little understood by Christian people in Britain today, perhaps because so many of us have given up fighting. We think that if a man disturbs people and is criticised, he must be wrong, forgetting that Christ was not crucified for being comfortable or 'top of the pops'. I remember a prince of the Anglican communion once asking me why a friend of mine was so fiercely hated 'even by some Christians'.

'The fact that he is hated,' I replied, 'does not prove that he is in the great Christian tradition. But if he were not hated at all—indeed by many—then he could not be.'

There was a long silence. 'Ah,' he said. 'The offence of the Cross.'

I said that I could not judge, but it might be so. One made many mistakes and was far from being the man one

132

ought to be. But it often seemed to be the few right things which one did, rather than one's mistakes, which provoked most gossip and fury.

When John Wesley first met persecution in Oxford, he was bewildered and asked his father what to do. Old Samuel, who had twice had his vicarage burnt down over his head—as much, some say, for his obstinacy as his piety—replied, 'I can scarcely think so meanly of you as that you would be discouraged with the "crackling of thorns under a pot"! Preserve an equal temper of mind under whatever treatment you meet with from a not very just or well-natured world.'

'Be steady,' old Samuel said to John and Charles later, on his deathbed. 'The Christian faith will surely revive in this kingdom. You shall see it though I shall not.'

Nothing seemed less probable at that moment. Yet Samuel's confidence was to be vindicated by the influence of Methodism, the Evangelical revival, the Oxford movement and the growth of the Catholic Church.

When you were translated to Canterbury, Dr Coggan, a distinguished bishop is said to have written that you were capable of bringing about within the Church of England a revolution as great as that achieved by Pope John in Rome. But the revolution required is, as you have seen, something far greater than a revolution in the Church. It needs to be the revolution whereby the Cross of Christ transforms not only all the Churches, but the nation and the world.

The Church of England, with its vast resources of property and manpower, obviously has a key part to play. What we need to seek together is a strategy adequate for the task.

The result must be in the hand of God, for as Wilberforce said at a difficult moment: 'God has given the very small increase there has been and must give all if there is to be more.' But experience shows that if people are united on what God wants them to do and on how they should do it, great things come to pass.

Yours sincerely,

Garth Lean.

5 *April 1975*
Oxford

References

CHAPTER 1

1: The Rev H A Williams: *Soundings* (Cambridge, 1962) pp 81f
2: *The Trial of Lady Chatterley* (Penguin, 1961) p 71 **3:** William
Belsen: *Juvenile Theft* (Harper and Rowe, 1975), reviewed in all
newspapers, 13 November 1975 **4:** *The Guardian*, 30 January
1976 **5:** 7 December 1975 **6:** Quoted from *Mount Ida* in
The New Morality (Blandford Press, 1964) **7:** Alexander Solzhenitsyn: *Nobel Speech*, and BBC Interview, 1 March 1976
8: Address to General Synod, 25 February 1976

CHAPTER 2

1: *The Daily Telegraph, 16 October 1975* **2:** Press release,
15 October 1975 **3:** *Catholic Herald*, 7 November 1975

CHAPTER 3

1: 5 November 1975 **2:** 12 October 1975 **3:** 16 October 1975
4: *The Times*, 22 October 1975 **5:** *The Times*, 24 November
1975 **6:** 8 May 1975 **7:** John Lawrence: *Take Hold of Change*
(SPCK, 1975) p 10 **8:** *The Guardian*, 8 February 1975 **9:**
Church Times, 5 December 1975 **10:** 17 October 1975

CHAPTER 4

1: Lecture to Royal Commonwealth Society, 8 October 1964
2: *The Times*, 13 November 1975 **3:** *Church Times*, 14 November 1975 **4:** Sermon in Great St Mary's, Cambridge, 9 November
1975. The Rev Paul Oestreicher, *Morning Star*, 11 November
1975 **5:** 2 November 1975 **6:** *Evening Argus*, Brighton, 4 December 1975 **7:** *The Daily Telegraph*, 16 July 1964 **8:** *Daily
Express*, 10 October 1962: *Christian Morals Now* (SCM, 1964)
p 15 **9:** L Tyerman: *Life and Times of John Wesley* (Hodder

and Stoughton, 1870) Vol 1, p 319   **10:** 1 November 1975
11: 1 November 1975   **12:** *The Times*, 1 December 1975   **13:** *The Longford Report* (Coronet Books, 1972) pp 188-191

CHAPTER 5

1: 2 November 1975   **2:** *Church Times*, 21 November 1975
3: Leonid Ilyichev, former Editor-in-Chief of *Pravda*, member of the Central Committee CPSU   **4:** From an extract from *Cancer Ward*, Vol 2 printed in *The Times*, 22 February 1969   **5:** 1 November 1975   **6:** Frank Buchman: *Remaking the World* (Blandford, 1958) p 172   **7:** *Evening Argus*, 4 December 1975   **8:** Malcolm Muggeridge: *Jesus* (Collins, 1975) p 131   **9:** Garth Lean: *John Wesley Anglican* (Blandford, 1964) p 110   **10:** *Morning Star*, 11 November 1975   **11:** Henry Drummond: *The Greatest Thing in the World* (Collins, 1930) pp 65-66

CHAPTER 6

1: For fuller treatment, see Lean: *Brave Men Choose* (Blandford, 1961)   **2:** Anstey: *The Atlantic Slave Trade and British Abolition* (Macmillan 1975) pp ix-xx, 52-3, 405-415   **3:** William Stewart: *J Keir Hardie* (Cassell, 1921) p 203

CHAPTER 7

1: For fuller treatment, see *Robert Carmichael par lui-meme* (Editions de Caux, 1975); Gabriel Marcel: *Fresh Hope for the World* (Longman, 1960) pp 118-126

CHAPTER 8

1: Cook, Lean: *The Black and White Book* (Blandford, 1972)
2: *The Times*, 21 November 1968   **3:** John 8, 11   **4:** e g Matthew 5, 24; Luke 19, 8   **5:** Peter Howard: *Britain and the Beast* (Heinemann, 1963) p 125   **6:** Theophil Spoerri: *Dynamik aus der Stille* (Caux-Verlag, Lucerne, 1971) p 29

CHAPTER 9

1: Address to the General Synod, 25 February 1976   **2:** Matthew 18, 20   **3:** *Church Times*, 30 January 1976   **4:** From an address on Palm Sunday, 1968, as published in *L'Osservatore Romano*   **5:** Donald Coggan: *The Prayers of the New Testament* (Hodder and Stoughton, 1967) pp 82-83   **6:** Acts 5, 20; 8, 29; 9, 11; 10, 3; 13, 2; 16, 6; 18, 9   **7:** Quoted in *The Sunday Times*, 7 December 1975, from *The Gulag Archipelago*, Vol II   **8:** L van der Post: *The Night of the New Moon* (Hogarth Press, 1970) pp 92-4   **9:** St Francis de Sales: *Introduction to the Devout Life*   **10:** *San Agostino, Soloqui*, (ed Antonio Marzulla, 1972)   **11:** A Gratry: *Les Sources de la Régéneration Sociale* (Paris, 1971) Chapter 1

CHAPTER 11

1: *Church Times*, 2 January 1976   **2:** *The Daily Telegraph*, 6 September 1974   **3:** *The Times*, 22 January 1976   **4:** *The Times*, 22 September 1969   **5:** *The Observer*, 23 October 1969   **6:** *The Sunday Times*, 20 July 1969   **7:** *Weekend Telegraph*, 30 September 1966   **8:** *The Sunday Telegraph*, 2 July 1967   **9:** P Hansford Johnson: *On Iniquity* (Macmillan, 1967) p 17   **10:** op cit p 33   **11:** *The Observer*, 11 December 1966   **12:** *The Observer*, 6 December 1965   **13:** 17 September 1967   **14:** *The Daily Telegraph*, 9 July 1973   **15:** *Daily Express*, 16 January 1976   **16:** *Evening Standard*, 15 January 1976   **17:** *The Guardian*, 16 January 1976   **18:** *Daily Express*, 16 January 1976   **19:** *The Observer*, 25 January 1976   **20:** *The Times*, 30 January 1976   **21:** *The Observer*, 1 February 1976   **22:** *The Times*, 7 February 1976   **23:** *Daily Express*, 28 August 1971   **24:** *The Observer*, 7 March 1971

CHAPTER 12

1: Platt, Hacker, Kenniston: *The Times*, 28 December 1970   **2:** *The Times*, 27 November 1967   **3:** Chaim Bernant: *The Walled Garden* (Weidenfeld and Nicolson, 1974) p 270   **4:** *Time*, 28 December 1970   **5:** *The Observer*, 22 December 1974   **6:** A Skulberg: *Education for Living* (Himmat, 1974)   **7:** Facts of this story have been checked with Filipino Government sources   **8:** *The Observer*, 12 January 1972

CHAPTER 13

1: 1 September 1975 **2:** 29 June 1975

CHAPTER 14

1: See e g *Storm of Crises*: a Study and Action Pack for World Development, sponsored by six UN agencies and the Government of the Netherlands. Produced by New Internationalist Publications Ltd, 1975 **2:** See e g United Nations World Food Conference 1974. *The World Food Problem*. Proposals for National and International Action E/CONF 65/4 **3:** Louis Emmerij, Director of the World Employment Programme, International Labour Organisation: *Workless of the World*, *New Internationalist*, No 32, October 1975 **4:** The New Economic Order; part of *Storm Crises* pack **5:** Exploding Cities Conference, Worcester College Oxford 1974, organised jointly by Harold Evans, Editor of *The Sunday Times*, and the UN fund for Population Activities **6:** See e g *Nuclear Thefts: Risks and Safeguards*. A report to the Energy Policy Project of the Ford Foundation by Prof Mason Willrich and Dr Theodore B Taylor; Ballinger Publishing Company, 1974 **7:** Barbara Ward and Rene Dubos, Andre Deutsch, 1972 **8:** Club of Rome **9:** Tarzie Vittachi, Executive Secretary, United Nations Fund for Population Activities **10:** FAO preparatory work for World Food Conference 1974 **11:** *Newsweek*, 11 November 1974 **12:** BBC TV, 18 March 1975 **13:** *The Daily Telegraph*, 17 November 1974 **14:** *Newsweek* op cit **15:** I G Patel, Deputy Administrator of the UN Development Programme. Address to the 44th Couchiching Conference, Geneva Park, Ontario Canada. Reported in *Action UNDP* Sept/Oct 1975 **16:** Conversation with Geoffrey Lean, May 1974 **17:** *The Times*, June 1972 **18:** *Yorkshire Post*, 26 August 1972 **19:** E F Schumacher: *Small is Beautiful* (Abacus, 1974) p 31, 32

CHAPTER 15

1: Lawrence: op cit, p 23 **2:** Buchman: op cit, p 162 **3:** op cit, p 147 **4:** John 16, 13 **5:** Hocking: *The Coming World Civilization* (Allen and Unwin, 1958) pp 166-167 **6:** *The Times*, 2 April 1976